REAL
MEXICAN

REAL
MEXICAN

FIONA DUNLOP

65 classic & contemporary recipes

Photography by Jean-Blaise Hall

MITCHELL BEAZLEY

An Hachette UK Company
www.hachette.co.uk

First published in Great Britain as *¡Viva La Revolucíon!* in
2008 by Mitchell Beazley, an imprint of Octopus Publishing
Group Ltd, Endeavour House, 189 Shaftesbury Avenue,
London WC2H 8JY

www.octopusbooks.co.uk

This edition published 2013 by Octopus Publishing Group

ISBN 978 1 84533 801 5

A CIP record for this book is available
from the British Library

Publisher Alison Starling
Art Director Jonathan Christie
Designer The Oak Studio
Photographer Jean-Blaise Hall
Recipe Translator Ana Sims
Project Editor Joanne Wilson
Assistant Production Manager Lucy Carter
Indexer Diana LeCore
Commissioning Editor for original edition Becca Spry
Editor for original edition Georgina Atsiaris, Debbie
Roberston

Printed and bound in China

CONTENTS

INTRODUCTION

Mexico has always thrived on radicalism, whether in political upheavals, sizzling colours or avant garde culture. Now it has turned to a gastronomic revamp. In the last few years a strengthening of national identity, or *Mexicanidad* (Mexican-ness) has propelled regional cooking back to centre stage, transforming the kitchens of top restaurants and those of country towns. This book, the result of long weeks travelling through Mexico, tracks those changes. Whether new or old, the recipes that follow all come straight from the heart of the country and its deep, ancient soul.

Rather than a revolution, it has been an evolution, bringing a complete reappraisal of food traditions that had come to be regarded as old-fashioned and even backward. From dynamic Mexico City to an eccentric hill village in Veracruz, to the towns of Morelia and Puebla, it encompasses the strongly indigenous Oaxaca valley and the Mayan territory in the Yucatán. In all there are 62 distinct indigenous groups, each with their own distinct cuisine.

Whether up in the dry sierra or down in the tropical coast, some of the tastiest local food is found in markets. From corn-based snacks such as *tostadas, tacos, chalupas, panuchos, esquites* and *uchepos,* to countless regional specialities. Today, refined versions of these classics grace the tablecloths of Mexico's

ritziest restaurants. Chillies are omnipresent, but their balance is being orchestrated more delicately. Tender *nopales* (cactus leaves) sneak into sophisticated salads, earthy *huitlacoche* (corn fungus) is revered as the Mexican truffle, *pepitas* (pumpkin seeds) adorn meats and silky yellow courgette flowers blossom *ad infinitum*.

As well as these there are the 'new' hallmarks of the herb-and-spice department: *hoja santa*, an aromatic leaf used to flavour or wrap fish and *tamales*; allspice berries; *amaranto* grains and leaves; dark red *achiote* seeds, and an indefinable herb, *epazote*. Chefs have eschewed more extreme native fauna such as armadillo (a pork-like meat still popular in the Isthmus and Chiapas) and iguana (found in Isthmus markets). They have embraced pre-Hispanic fowl and game such as duck, turkey and venison, moving away from the Old World stalwarts of beef, lamb and pork.

Desserts, other than the cake and sweet production of the convents, were never a Mexican forte as sugar had no place in the indigenous diet, but even that is changing. Nor can you sing the praises of Mexico's beers too highly, from sunny Corona to golden Pacifico to the dark Yucatecan brew, León. Then there are the smooth, upgraded tequilas and, hard on their heels, estate-bottled *mezcales*. Mexico's palate-tantalizing riches seem infinite.

The world's first fusion food

The Spaniards landed in Veracruz in 1519 a few decades after the Moors' 800-year-long occupation of Spain ended. The Moorish imprint was still evident in the spices, citrus fruit and rice that were brought to Mexico. Imports adapted well; cattle for meat and dairy products, wheat, sugar cane, apples, onions and herbs all flourished.

Then a vital change occurred with pork, bringing lard and frying: a departure for the indigenous Mexicans. Until then cooking involved boiling, steaming or, for the Mayas, smoking and baking in underground pits. Instead of salt the mineral *tequesquite* was added.

From sugar came sweets and cakes, something the nuns of Puebla excelled at when not labouring over their complex *moles,* and from Seville oranges came Yucatecan marinades. Further foreign input came when Spanish galleons sailed directly across the Pacific to unload Oriental bounty at Acapulco. Sesame seeds, cinnamon, garlic and coriander were all introduced through this back door. In reverse, Mexico gave Old Europe chillies, tomatoes, avocadoes, pumpkins, turkey, vanilla and, of course, chocolate, that divine tipple supped by the Aztec emperor Moctezuma from a cup of solid gold after a typical 30-course dinner. With all these riches, Mexican cuisine is a revelation. It is an assault of subtle, smoky, sometimes fiery

but always exotic flavours and textures that are completely foreign to Old World palates and light-years from Tex-Mex. Flour is hardly ever used for making sauces; in its place there are salsas, *moles* or *pipianes* (rich, complex, thickened purées), *adobos* (sour marinades) and *recados* (Mayan seasoning). In fact, Mexican cooking is considered to be one of the world's three original cuisines, along with those of China and France.

It was first talked of by Bernardino de Sahagun (1499–1590), a Franciscan missionary who, after becoming fluent in Nahuatl, the language of the Aztecs, compiled the *Florentine Codex*. This documented Aztec society and culture. Other observations came from Bernal Díaz (1496–1584), a captain in the army of Hernán Cortés and author of *The Conquest of New Spain* (1568). More recently the theorist José Iturriaga de la Fuente headed a massive state-funded investigation into Mexico's regional market food. And Laura Esquivel's magic-realist book *Like Water for Chocolate* (1989) and film (1992) did much to romanticize Mexican cuisine. Who can forget Tita's lovingly prepared quail with rose petals?

Corn worship

Some things just do not change. Take corn (maize), thought to have been cultivated from wild grass 6000–7000 years ago. For all Mexicans, corn is sacred: well over 300 million corn *tortillas* are consumed daily (not counting the wheat ones in northern Mexico). The Mayas believed man was made of corn while the Mexicas (ancestors of the Aztecs) said their god of corn, Centéotl, was born in Michoacán, 'land of water and humidity'. *Tortillas* ('little cakes') were named as such by the Spaniards. Vital but labour-intensive energy-givers, they are estimated to have monopolised 35–40 hours a week of a pre-Hispanic woman's time. No Aztec man would be seen dead with a *metate* and *mano* (lava stone rolling table and rolling pin) or *molcajete* and *tejolote* (mortar and pestle), the unrivalled kitchen equipment that are still widely used.

CHILLIES

Chillies, the secret weapon

Mexican cuisine is often perceived as chilli-hot in the extreme. This is rarely the case: when the heat of a chilli, such as the *habanero*, comes close to shooting off the Scoville scale (the universal measure of capsaicin, or chilli fieriness), it is incorporated into a salsa, so it can be carefully rationed. What is true is that chillies are addictive: once tasted, never forgotten. Some 200 varieties exist but the most common ones boil down to a dozen or so, including *ancho, mulato* and *pasilla,* the holy trinity of *moles.* Mexican cooks are adept at building up complex flavours by combining different varieties or by blending fresh, dried and smoked chillies. Each region has its favourite chillies and, like corn, some are unique to one area. To confuse matters further, names change according to whether the chillies are fresh, smoked and/or dried: a dried *poblano* chilli, for example, becomes an *ancho,* and the popular *chipotle* is really a smoked and dried *jalapeño.* Like Mexico's other primary foods, the chilli goes back thousands of years.

Instinctive nutrition

The native Mexican diet had remarkable nutritional balance. For example, the amino acid levels in corn and beans complement each other perfectly; *nopales* (cactus leaves) contain abundant vitamins A, C, B complex and iron;

and avocados contribute nearly 20 different vitamins and minerals. Fresh chillies have plenty of vitamin C; dried ones vitamin A. *Amaranto* seed, a 'superfood' packed with protein, calcium, iron, vitamin E and lycine, had great ritualistic significance for the Aztecs. Even the hallowed *masa harina* (corn flour), the basis of *tortillas,* is bursting with calcium after the corn kernels have been soaked then slow-cooked with lime or wood ash. Fresh fruit juices mixed on street corners are now an art in themselves. In view of this, it is doubly tragic that Mexico is now the world's greatest consumer of Coca-Cola, with the Yucatán top of the class. Compare that with the vitamin C rich *agua de jamaica* (hibiscus flower juice).

Today's *nueva cocina* is fighting a tough battle against processed and convenience products, mainly imported from the US and the globalized markets. Yet with innovative, energetic chefs from Mexico City to Michoacán, Puebla to Veracruz and Oaxaca to the Yucatán leading the way, the word is spreading. Regional food is more popular than ever and has become emperor again, although with completely transformed presentation and an inimitable Mexican touch: poetry, magic, the whisper of the gods? But ultimately, when you stand on a street-corner, sniff the air and scent that unmistakable aroma of corn, whether from *tacos*, *elotes* or *tostadas*, you know for sure you are in Mexico.

APERITIVOS, SALSAS Y LADOS

SNACKS, SAUCES & SIDES

GUACAMOLE NACIONALISTA
'NATIONALIST' GUACAMOLE

The colours of this dish represent the beloved Mexican flag: green, red and white. The pomegranate ping makes a great addition to this classic starter. The dish is easy to make and will keep in the fridge for a few hours covered in clingfilm to avoid discolouring. Serve with *tortilla* chips or toasted pita bread.

SERVES 6

2 large onions, peeled and finely chopped

425ml (15fl oz) fresh lemon juice

4 large avocados, about 850g (1lb 14oz), peeled and stoned

115g (4oz) chopped fresh coriander leaves

85g (3oz) *serrano* chillies, deseeded, deveined and chopped

salt and freshly ground black pepper

30g (1oz) fresh pomegranate seeds

55g (2oz) ricotta, crumbled

Marinate the onion in the lemon juice for half an hour, then drain and set aside.

Mash the avocado and add the coriander, marinated onion and *serrano* chillies. Season with salt and pepper.

Make a mound of guacamole on a serving plate and scatter over the pomegranate seeds and ricotta.

FRIJOLES RANCHEROS
SPICY BEANS

A tasty way to stave off hunger pangs, this dish can be served as an accompaniment with meat or eaten with eggs for breakfast, Mexican-style. Cooking times for beans vary, so just test the softness.

SERVES 4

500g (1lb 2oz) pinto beans, soaked overnight or for at least 10 hours

1 tbsp vegetable oil

100g (3½oz) streaky bacon, cut into pieces

2–3 *jalapeño* chillies, sliced lengthways

1 medium onion, peeled and thinly sliced

salt, to taste

100g (3½oz) strong cheese, such as Parmesan or mature Cheddar, grated

Drain off the soaking water from the beans then tip them into a large saucepan. Cover with cold water, bring to the boil and simmer for at least 2 hours until soft. Drain and set aside.

Heat the oil in a frying pan then add the bacon. As soon as it starts to crisp, tip in the chillies and onion and fry for a further 10–15 minutes. Add the beans and salt. Cook for a few more minutes to heat the beans through. Serve piping hot, sprinkled with grated cheese.

RAVIOL DE AGUACATE RELLENO

PRAWN-FILLED AVOCADO RAVIOLI

Delicate but with a strong kick from the chilli mayonnaise, these avocado 'sandwiches' are pure heaven!

SERVES 4

2½ tbsp butter

1 small onion, peeled and finely diced

1 garlic clove, peeled and crushed

1 kg (2lb 4oz) prawns (about 21–25), cleaned and cut into thirds

1 small potato, peeled and diced

1 small carrot, peeled and diced

small bunch fresh coriander, chopped

1 *serrano* chilli, chopped

salt, to taste

2 large ripe Hass avocados

½ red onion, peeled and cut into strips, to garnish

zest from 2 lemons, chopped, to garnish

fleur de sel or coarse sea salt and black pepper

FOR THE CHIPOTLE MAYONNAISE & GREEN OIL

200ml (7fl oz) vegetable oil

1 egg yolk

1 tsp fresh lemon juice

1 tbsp Dijon mustard

25g (1oz) *chipotle* chilli pulp

small bunch of fresh coriander

50ml (2fl oz) corn oil

Melt the butter in a saucepan and sauté the onion and garlic until softened. Add the prawns, quickly sauté to seal the juices, then cover and cook over low heat for about 7 minutes. Drain, reserving the liquid. Once the mixture has cooled, briefly mince it in a food processor and set aside in a bowl.

Boil the potato and carrot in a little water until just tender. Drain, allow to cool and mix with the prawns. Stir in the coriander, the chilli and enough of the reserved prawn juices to moisten without becoming sloppy. Add salt to taste and set aside.

To make the mayonnaise, blend together the oil, egg yolk, lemon juice, mustard and salt in a food processor – alternatively use about 200ml (7fl oz) of a good-quality bought mayonnaise – then stir in the *chipotle* chilli pulp. Set aside in the refrigerator and make the green oil. Quickly blanch the coriander in salted boiling water, then plunge into iced water to cool. Drain. Put into a blender or food processor with the oil and salt and whiz until intensely green and very smooth.

Just before serving, cut the avocados in half, remove the stones, and slice thinly lengthways. Place three slices side by side on each serving plate, then put a spoonful of prawn filling on each. Cover with three more slices of avocado.

Top each 'ravioli' with a dollop of spicy mayonnaise and garnish with some onion strips and a scattering of lemon zest. Finish with a swirl of green oil, a sprinkling of *fleur de sel* and a twist of freshly ground pepper.

CEVICHE DE CAMARONES EN AGUACHILE
MARINATED CHILLI PRAWNS

This beautiful dish has a delicate air about it that is completely belied by the heat of the chilli. Although *jalapeño* is one of the milder types, you may want to reduce the quantity. This makes a perfect starter for a hot summer's day – washed down with a cool Mexican beer.

SERVES 4

600g (1lb 5oz) large raw prawns, cleaned and butterflied

700ml (1¼ pints) fresh lemon juice

375g (13oz) cucumber, peeled, deseeded and thinly sliced into semicircles

12 jalapeño chillies, deseeded, deveined and cut into strips

1 red onion, peeled and chopped into thin strips

salt and freshly ground black pepper

Place the prawns in a non-metallic bowl and pour over the lemon juice. Add the remaining ingredients, season with salt and pepper, and leave to marinate for 15 minutes.

Serve with savoury Mexican-style crackers or toast.

CHALUPAS

TORTILLA AND SPICY BEEF SNACKS

Walk around the corner from Puebla's *Mesón de la Sacristía* and you may find a stout little lady on a street corner turning out *chalupas* until late at night. Clubbers love them. Typical of Pueblan street food, they make tasty little snacks or starters, but should be crisp and freshly made.

Fry the *tortillas,* 1 or 2 at a time, in some oil on both sides until crisp. Without removing them from the pan, place a tablespoon of chilli sauce on top of each one, alternating colours. Top with some onion and shredded beef. Serve immediately.

SERVES 4
----

8 small corn *tortillas,* about 10cm (4in) in diameter

vegetable oil

250ml (8fl oz) green chilli sauce

250ml (8fl oz) red chilli sauce

1 small onion, peeled and finely diced

250g (9oz) shredded cooked beef

TRADITIONAL *MOLE POBLANO*

Dried *mulato, ancho* and *pasilla* chillies are all available by mail order. *Mulato* and *ancho* chillies are similar in flavour, except that the *mulato* is slightly sweeter, while the *pasilla* is much punchier. Although far from having the legendary 20–30 ingredients, this *mole poblano* tastes like the real McCoy. Serve it with any meat or vegetable of your choice.

SERVES 4–5

vegetable oil

3 *mulato* chillies, stems and seeds removed

3 *ancho* chillies, stems and seeds removed

3 *pasilla* chillies, stems and seeds removed

500g (1lb 2oz) tomatoes

200g (7oz) peeled and roughly chopped onion

2 garlic cloves, peeled

1 plantain, peeled (soak in warm water for 15 minutes to aid peeling) and chopped

1 corn *tortilla*

225ml (8fl oz) chicken stock

90g (3¼oz) dark chocolate (70% cocoa), broken into small pieces

100g (3½oz) dark soft brown sugar

Heat 5cm (2in) vegetable oil in a deep saucepan. When hot, fry the chillies until crisp. Remove and lay on paper towels to absorb the excess oil. Save the oil.

Grill the tomatoes, onion and garlic on a hot griddle or under a hot grill, turning frequently to brown on all sides.

Put the chillies and grilled tomatoes, onion and garlic in a large saucepan and pour in 1 litre (1¾ pints) of water. Bring to the boil, then reduce the heat and simmer for about 10 minutes or until the chillies are soft.

Blend the vegetables and cooking liquid together in a food processor to make a sauce. Strain and set aside.

Fry the plantain in the reserved oil until lightly browned.

Toast the *tortilla* on both sides under a grill until completely blackened.

Blend the plantain and *tortilla* together with some water in a food processor. Strain to form a smooth sauce and set aside.

Bring the chilli sauce to the boil in a saucepan and cook for about 10 minutes. Then stir in the plantain sauce and the chicken stock. Add the chocolate and sugar, bring to the boil and simmer for 45 minutes or until thickened.

MOLE SACRISTÍA
SMOKY SACRISTÍA *MOLE*

Tomatillos have a tart flavour which makes them an invaluable ingredient. The main flavour of this simplified *mole* comes from the strong, smoky *chipotle* chilli, which is in fact a dried and smoked *jalapeño* chilli with a lingering heat – some would say burn. It is delicious with organic chicken, pork or even grilled fish.

SERVES 4–5

500g (1lb 2oz) *tomatillos,* fresh or canned

2 onions, peeled and roughly chopped

1 garlic clove, peeled

3 *chipotle* chillies

1 tbsp vegetable oil

250ml (9fl oz) chicken stock

salt, to taste

Grill the *tomatillos*, onion and garlic on a hot griddle or under a hot grill, turning frequently to brown on all sides.

Fry the *chipotle* chillies in the oil until they turn golden brown.

Blend the tomato, onion, garlic and chillies together in a blender or food processor with a little water to form a smooth purée. Pour the purée into a saucepan and simmer over a low heat for 10 minutes. Add enough chicken stock to form a thick sauce, heat through and season with salt.

PIPIÁN VERDE

GREEN PUMPKIN SEED SAUCE

This sumptuous green sauce can be served with poultry or with pork. Sauces thickened with pumpkin seeds were used extensively by the Mayas and later the Aztecs.

SERVES 4–5

500g (1lb 2oz) tomatillos, fresh or canned

3 large onions, peeled and halved

2 garlic cloves, peeled

40g (1½oz) *serrano* or *jalapeño* chillies, deseeded, deveined and roughly chopped

bunch of fresh coriander, leaves only

bunch of fresh *epazote* (optional)

225g (8oz) hulled pumpkin seeds

1 tbsp vegetable oil

250ml (9fl oz) chicken stock

salt, to taste

Grill the *tomatillos*, onion, garlic and chillies on a griddle or under a hot grill, turning frequently to brown on all sides.

Put the grilled *tomatillos*, onion, garlic and chillies in a blender or food processor and add the coriander, *epazote* and 250ml (9fl oz) of water. Whizz until well blended and set aside.

Fry the pumpkin seeds in the oil until golden, then reduce to crumbs in a coffee grinder. Mix the crumbs with 250ml (9fl oz) of water and cook in a saucepan over a medium heat for 2 minutes.

Put the pumpkin seed mixture and chilli sauce into a saucepan and mix together. Bring to the boil, add the chicken stock, season with salt and simmer, uncovered, for about 15 minutes until thickened.

MOSAICO DE BERENJENA Y QUESO DE CABRA
AUBERGINE AND GOAT'S CHEESE MOSAIC

Relatively easy to prepare, yet spiked with contrasting flavours, this vegetarian terrine makes a great summer starter or informal lunch. The aubergine was brought to Mexico by the Spaniards, but red peppers are truly indigenous. Advance salting helps reduce the amount of oil the aubergine absorbs during cooking.

SERVES 6

3 large aubergines, about 700g (1lb 9oz)

salt, to taste

2 tbsp olive oil

225g (8oz) soft goat's cheese

1½ tbsp single cream

3 red peppers, about 325g (11½ oz), roasted, peeled, deseeded and cut into strips

6 sprigs of fresh mint, to garnish

FOR THE PARSLEY SAUCE

8 tbsp fresh flat-leaf parsley leaves

100ml (3½fl oz) olive oil

1 garlic clove, peeled

Peel the aubergines and cut them lengthways into thin slices. Salt on both sides and lay on paper towels for at least 15 minutes until liquid seeps out. Rinse and pat dry.

Gently fry the aubergine slices in a little olive oil until golden brown, then lay them on paper towels to absorb the excess oil.

Beat the cheese and cream together until smooth.

Line a deep ovenproof dish or 450g (1lb) loaf tin, about 9cm × 12cm × 7cm (3½in × 4½in × 2¾in), with clingfilm, leaving some hanging over the sides. Place a layer of aubergine at the bottom, then a layer of red peppers and over that spread a layer of creamy cheese. Repeat layers in the same order to fill the dish, ending with a layer of aubergine. Press down firmly, cover with the cling film and refrigerate for at least 2 hours.

To make the parsley sauce, whiz all the ingredients in a blender or food processor.

To serve, carefully remove the terrine from the dish and cut into slices about 2cm (¾in) thick. Place one slice on each plate, drizzle with the parsley sauce and garnish with a sprig of mint.

SOPAS

SOUPS

CREMA FRÍA DE AGUACATE CON SEMILLA

CHILLED CREAM OF AVOCADO SOUP

You will have never tasted a dish like this before. Aromatic herbs contrast with hot chilli, subtle avocado and coconut. Use plain desiccated coconut if you can't find the chilli version. For a sharper flavour, add a spoonful of white wine vinegar.

SERVES 4–6

In a food processor, blend the avocado, chillies, soured cream, coconut milk and chicken stock. Add the coriander seeds, oregano and salt to taste. Strain and refrigerate until chilled.

To make the sweet potato fritters, heat 1cm (½in) of oil in a frying pan over a high heat. When the oil is hot, add the sweet potato slices and reduce heat to medium. Slowly fry the sweet potato slices until just golden and slightly crisp. Remove from the oil and lay on paper towels to absorb the excess oil.

To make the oregano vinaigrette, whisk the vinegar with the mustard and season with salt and pepper. Add the dried oregano, then the olive oil and beat to blend well.

Serve the chilled soup in individual bowls, topped with a splash of oregano vinaigrette, diced apple and cucumber, a couple of sweet potato fritters and a sprinkling of chilli-flavoured coconut.

2 large avocados, about 450g (1lb), peeled and stoned

1½ *serrano* chillies

2 tbsp soured cream

100ml (3½fl oz) coconut milk

300ml (10fl oz) chicken stock

1½ tsp coriander seeds, crushed

1 tsp dried oregano

salt, to taste

1 large green apple, cored and diced

55g (2oz) cucumber, peeled and diced

1 tbsp chilli-flavoured desiccated coconut

FOR THE SWEET POTATO FRITTERS

1 sweet potato, peeled and thinly sliced

vegetable, corn or peanut oil

FOR THE OREGANO VINAIGRETTE

2 tbsp white wine vinegar

1 tsp Dijon mustard

salt and finely ground white pepper

2 tsp dried oregano

1 tbsp finely chopped fresh oregano (or sage)

125ml (4fl oz) olive oil

SOPA DE CAMOTE Y PECHUGA

SWEET POTATO AND CHICKEN SOUP

Sweet potatoes were brought to Mexican shores by the Spaniards from West Africa via the Caribbean islands. This particular recipe originated in Querétaro, in the Bajio, north of Mexico City. The soft, sweet pulp combines deliciously with the chicken using an unusual technique.

SERVES 6

500g (1lb 2oz) sweet potatoes

250g (9oz) skinned chicken breast

2 egg yolks

3 tbsp butter

½ tsp nutmeg

2 allspice berries, ground

1.5 litres (3 pints) hot chicken stock

salt and freshly ground black pepper

3 tbsp finely chopped fresh coriander

Preheat the oven to 180°C/350°F/Gas 4.

Wash and dry the sweet potatoes and place in a baking tin. Cover with kitchen foil and bake for about 30 minutes or until the potatoes are tender when pierced with a pointed knife. Remove from the oven and leave to cool a little, then peel and mash, removing any coarse fibres.

In a food processor, chop up the chicken quite finely. Add the chicken to the sweet potato with the egg yolks, butter, nutmeg and allspice. Mix well and season with salt to taste. The mixture should have a thick, dumpling-like texture.

Turn the mixture out onto a work surface. Pat out until 1cm (½in) thick and shape into rectangles about 8cm (3¼in) wide, then cut into strips measuring about 2cm × 8cm (¾in × 3¼in).

Bring some water to the boil in a large saucepan, add a little salt and drop in the strips. Cook for about 20 minutes. Carefully remove the strips from the water with a slotted spoon, drain in a colander, and place in a soup tureen or distribute between individual soup bowls.

Pour the hot chicken stock over the strips and sprinkle with freshly ground black pepper and finely chopped coriander. Serve immediately.

SUQUET DE ALCACHOFA CON ALMEJAS
ARTICHOKE AND CLAM SOUP

At Naos in Mexico City this rich, creamy soup, full of subtle flavours, is served as a starter, but it could easily become a main course. If fresh artichoke hearts are unavailable, use frozen ones.

SERVES 4

2 large garlic cloves, peeled and thinly sliced

3 tbsp olive oil

1.25kg (2lb 12oz) fresh clams (about 20), shells scrubbed clean

8 sprigs of fresh thyme

125ml (4fl oz) white wine

4 fresh artichoke hearts, about 300g (10½oz), cleaned and cut into eighths

850ml (1½ pints) fish stock

salt and freshly ground black pepper

¼ tsp chicken bouillon powder

400ml (14fl oz) fresh double cream

1 tbsp chopped fresh chives

fennel fronds, to garnish

FOR THE BEURRE MANIÉ

20g (¾oz) butter, at room temperature

20g (¾oz) plain flour

Rinse the clams and discard any with open shells which fail to close when they are tapped on the side of the sink.

In a deep saucepan, sauté the garlic in the olive oil until golden, then add the clams, thyme and white wine. Cover and cook for 3–5 minutes.

Add the artichoke hearts and the fish stock, season with salt, pepper and chicken boullion powder, then simmer, uncovered, until the liquid has reduced to a quarter of its original volume. Discard any clams with closed shells.

To make the *beurre manié*, mix the butter and flour to a smooth paste and then form into four balls with your fingers.

Add the cream and the *beurre manié* balls to the soup, stirring continuously until well blended and thickened.

Serve hot in bowls, sprinkled with chives and fennel fronds.

CREMA DE FRIJOL
CREAM OF BEAN SOUP

Black beans are quintessentially Mexican, particularly popular among the Mayas. Serve this simple soup garnished with fried *chipotle* chillis and cubes of fresh goat's cheese.

SERVES 4–6

450g (1lb) black beans, soaked in water overnight

1 small onion, peeled and quartered

salt, to taste

3 tbsp vegetable oil

1 small onion, finely chopped

Drain the soaked beans and place them in a large saucepan. Add enough water to cover them and add the onion.

Bring to the boil, reduce the heat and simmer slowly for about 2 hours, or until the beans are softened. Whiz the beans with their cooking liquid in a blender.

Heat the oil in a large saucepan and fry the chopped onion until golden. Add the bean mixture, bring to the boil and add 1 litre (1¾ pints) of water and salt to taste. Simmer for 3 minutes until heated through.

SOPA TARASCA

TARASCAN CHILLI BEAN SOUP

From Michoacán comes a wholesome Tarascan soup combining classic flavours with a scattering of *tortilla* strips (like *Sopa Azteca*), cheese and avocado. Vary the quantities to make the soup more or less filling.

SERVES 4–6

6 corn tortillas, cut into short strips

peanut or corn oil

3 ancho chillies, cut into strips

200g (7oz) tomatoes, deseeded and roughly chopped

1 small onion, peeled and roughly chopped

2 garlic cloves, peeled

250g (9oz) beans (any type except black), cooked and puréed

2 litres (3½ pints) chicken stock

salt, to taste

250ml (9fl oz) crème fraîche

250g (9oz) firm, fresh cheese like mozarella, cut into small cubes

1 large avocado, peeled, stoned and sliced lengthways

Fry the *tortilla* strips in a little oil until crisp. Remove, lay on paper towels to absorb any excess oil and set aside.

Lightly fry the *ancho* chilli strips in a little oil.

In a food processor, blend the tomatoes, onion, garlic and fried *ancho* chilli strips, reserving a handful of strips for garnishing, to a smooth purée. Set aside.

Blend the bean purée, half the *tortilla* strips and the chicken stock in a food processor. Pour this and the tomato mixture into a saucepan, stir well, season with salt and simmer with a lid on for about 10 minutes.

Serve hot in individual soup bowls, topped with a spoonful of crème fraîche and accompanied by a plate of cheese cubes, the remaining *tortilla* and *ancho* chilli strips and the avocado slices.

CALDO DE MARISCOS
SEAFOOD BROTH

Rumoured to cure any sailor's hangover, this soup is pure comfort, packed with tangy flavour and hot chilli. The most important stage is the correct preparation of the broth and the *jalapeño* chillies. Use any seafood you wish, but make sure it is fresh.

SERVES 4

1 tbsp olive oil

1 large onion, peeled and chopped

2 *jalapeño* chillies, deseeded, deveined and sliced, or 55g (2oz) canned *jalapeños* in *escabeche* (pickled chillies)

2 garlic cloves, peeled and crushed

3 medium tomatoes, deseeded and chopped

bunch of fresh coriander, leaves only, finely chopped

1 bay leaf

salt, to taste

400g (14oz) fresh raw prawns, shelled

300g (10½oz) fresh raw crayfish

600–700g (1lb 5oz–1lb 9oz) trout fillet, cut into chunks

juice of 1 lime

Heat the oil in a large saucepan, then add the onion, *jalapeño* chillies, garlic and tomatoes. Fry over a low heat until the onion has softened and the tomato has become a pulp.

Add 1 litre (1¾ pints) of water, the coriander, bay leaf and some salt. Cover with a lid and slowly bring to the boil. Carefully drop the seafood and trout into the broth and simmer with the lid on for 10 minutes or until cooked all the way through.

Before serving, remove the bay leaf and add the lime juice.

SOPA MESTIZA
MESTIZO SOUP

In Mexican, the word *mestizo* crops up again and again, referring to people of mixed Spanish and indigenous blood. Here it is applied to a nourishing soup of mixed vegetables, made truly Mexican by a fiery edge of *chipotle* chillies.

Heat the oil in large saucepan and sauté the leeks, celery, carrots, onions, mushrooms, sweetcorn, courgette flowers and garlic until tender.

Add the tomatoes, chillies, *epazote* and chicken stock and bring to the boil. Add salt to taste, and serve piping hot.

SERVES 6

2 tbsp vegetable oil

70g (2½oz) each of chopped leeks, celery and carrots

1 small onion, peeled and roughly chopped

25g (1oz) mushrooms, sliced

40g (1½oz) cooked sweetcorn kernels, fresh or canned

40g (1½oz) courgette flowers, rinsed

2 garlic cloves, peeled and crushed

1kg (2lb 4oz) tomatoes, skinned and finely chopped

1 tsp chopped canned *chipotle* chillies

1 tsp fresh chopped *epazote* or 1 tbsp flat-leaf parsley

1.7 litres (3 pints) chicken stock

salt, to taste

SOPA DE LIMA
LIME AND CHICKEN BROTH

It is impossible not to become hooked on this divine, piquant broth, an absolute classic of the Yucatán peninsula that has now travelled far afield. The Hacienda Teya version is one of the best.

SERVES 6

1–2 skinned chicken breasts, about 300g (10½oz) in total

1 whole garlic bulb, peeled

1 sprig of fresh oregano

small bunch of fresh coriander

salt, to taste

2 tbsp corn oil

450g (1lb) onions, peeled and roughly chopped

400g (14oz) green peppers, deseeded and chopped

200g (7oz) tomatoes, chopped

juice of 6 limes

2 chicken stock cubes

4 soft corn tortillas, cut in thin strips and lightly fried

2 limes, thinly sliced

Pour 2 litres (3¼ pints) of water into a large saucepan and add the chicken breasts, garlic, oregano and coriander and salt. Bring to the boil over a high heat then turn the heat down to low–medium and simmer for about 30 minutes or until the chicken is cooked.

Remove the chicken from the broth, shred and set aside. Strain the broth and set aside.

Heat the oil in a large saucepan and sauté the onions, peppers and tomatoes over a low heat until softened. Then pour in the strained chicken broth, add the lime juice and crumble in the stock cubes. Simmer for 10 minutes, then strain the broth again.

To serve, place some shredded chicken, a few *tortilla* strips and a slice or two of lime in individual serving bowls, then pour over the hot chicken broth.

CONSOMMÉ PARA UN ENFERMO
RESTORATIVE CHICKEN CONSOMMÉ

Unbelievably comforting stuff on a cold winter's day, this soup warms the cockles and does not take long to make.

SERVES 6

2 chicken breasts, skinned
1 medium onion, peeled
1 garlic clove, peeled
1 tsp salt
4 tbsp freshly cooked long-grain rice
5 *serrano* chillies, seeded and minced
1 small onion, peeled and finely chopped
bunch of fresh coriander, chopped
avocado slices, to garnish

In a large saucepan, simmer the chicken breasts in 2 litres (3½ pints) of water with the onion, garlic and salt, covered, for 30 minutes or until the chicken is cooked through. Remove the chicken breasts, cool and shred coarsely.

Strain the stock into a clean saucepan and add the shredded chicken, rice, chillies and onion. Simmer with the lid on for 10 minutes. Serve immediately, garnished with avocado slices.

SOPA DE HABAS

BROAD BEAN SOUP

With flavours that far surpass its humble name, this soup is a multi-layered concoction by Oaxacan chef Alejandro Ruiz. Like chickpeas, broad beans are not native to Mexico but started life in the Middle East.

SERVES 4

2 tbsp vegetable oil

1 small onion, peeled and finely chopped

1 garlic clove, peeled and crushed

2 tomatoes, chopped

400g (14oz) dried broad beans, (yellow in colour) cooked in salted water

200g (7oz) cooked chickpeas, skinned, or canned

200g (7oz) corn kernels, cooked in salted water, or canned

16 medium dried prawns

1 litre (1¾ pints) fish consommé or water

salt and freshly ground black pepper

2 tbsp chopped fresh coriander, to garnish

In a large saucepan, heat the oil and sauté the onion and garlic for about 1 minute. Add the tomatoes and cook for a couple of minutes over a low heat.

Mash the tomatoes with a fork then add the beans, chickpeas, corn, prawns and fish consommé. Bring to the boil, reduce the heat and simmer for about 10 minutes. Season with salt and pepper to taste and garnish with a sprinkling of coriander.

CREMA DE CILANTRO
CREAM OF CORIANDER SOUP

Creamy, subtle and pungent, this is a great new take on vegetable soup. It can be served with croutons.

SERVES 6

8 tbsp butter

2 garlic cloves, peeled and finely chopped

1 onion, peeled and finely chopped

1 small green pepper, deseeded and finely chopped

1 small leek, finely chopped

3 celery stalks, finely chopped

2 carrots, finely chopped

3 tbsp plain flour

2 litres (3¼ pints) milk

3 bay leaves

3 small bunches of fresh coriander, very finely chopped

2 chicken stock cubes

Melt the butter in a large saucepan and sweat the garlic, onion and vegetables over a low heat until softened. Stir the flour into the juices and continue stirring while pouring in 1 litre of the milk and adding the bay leaves.

Stir the coriander into the remaining milk and pour into the saucepan. Crumble in the stock cubes. Bring to the boil and simmer for 5 minutes until the soup thickens, then strain and serve immediately.

MARISCO

SEAFOOD

TRUCHA VERACRUZANA
VERACRUZ-STYLE TROUT

This is Xico-based chef Flor Patricia Perez's quick-fix trout recipe – a healthy dish that makes full use of an abundance of local river trout. It is a shortened version of the famous Veracruz recipe for *huachinango* (red snapper). You could use salmon instead of the trout.

SERVES 2

55g (2oz) pitted green olives, roughly chopped

55g (2oz) capers with their pickling juice

4 medium plum tomatoes, chopped

1 medium onion, peeled and roughly chopped

2 garlic cloves, peeled and crushed

1 tsp dried oregano

1 tsp dried thyme

2 large trout fillets

Put all the ingredients, except the trout, in a large saucepan and cook together over a low heat for about 8–10 minutes until softened.

Lay the trout fillets carefully in the sauce, cover with a lid, and leave to cook gently for 10 minutes or until cooked through. Serve immediately.

ATÚN EN SALSA DE SOJA

TUNA WITH SOY SAUCE

This divine fusion dish mixes Asian-derived flavour of soy sauce with North African citrus juice and typically Mexican courgette flowers. It should be served immediately, with steamed white rice and sliced fresh tomatoes.

SERVES 4

50ml (2fl oz) olive oil

800g (1lb 12oz) fresh tuna, cut into 4 equal fillets

12 garlic cloves, peeled and crushed

250ml (9fl oz) soy sauce

125ml (4fl oz) fresh lemon juice

100ml (3½fl oz) fresh orange juice

100g (3½oz) butter

4 courgette flowers, rinsed (optional)

In a large frying pan, heat the olive oil, then quickly sear the tuna fillets on a high heat for 1 minute on each side. Add the garlic and fry for 30 seconds until just golden. Pour in the soy sauce and the fruit juices, then remove the tuna from the frying pan and set aside.

Lower the heat and continue to cook the sauce for another minute until all the ingredients are well blended and the sauce is slightly reduced, then stir in the butter.

Place the tuna fillets on individual plates then, if available dip the courgette flowers in the soy sauce mixture and place one on top of each fillet. Bathe the tuna with the remaining sauce.

FILETE DE PESCADO AL LIMÓN CON ALCAPARRAS Y FLOR DE CALABAZA

FISH FILLET WITH LEMON, CAPERS AND COURGETTE FLOWERS

The crisp skin and soft flesh of the fish contrasts beautifully with the sauce with its sharp bite of capers and lemon. The big surprise here is the sweet tomato marmalade.

SERVES 4

FOR THE FISH FILLETS

4 red snapper or grouper fillets, about 200g (7oz) each

salt and freshly ground black pepper

1 small garlic clove, peeled and crushed

5 tbsp olive oil

55g (2oz) capers

55ml (2fl oz) fresh lemon juice

85g (3oz) butter

12 courgette flowers, rinsed

FOR THE TOMATO MARMALADE

800g (1lb 12oz) tomatoes, skinned, quartered and deseeded

2 tbsp runny honey

2 tbsp olive oil

1 sprig of fresh rosemary

salt and freshly ground pepper

First prepare the marmalade. Preheat the oven to 200°C/400°F/Gas 6. Place the tomatoes in a roasting tin, pour over the honey and olive oil, add the rosemary and season with salt and pepper. Roast for 45 minutes.

Remove the tomatoes from the oven. If any juice remains, boil over a high heat until any liquid has evaporated. Set aside.

Season the fish fillets with salt and pepper and rub over the garlic. Heat the olive oil in a frying pan. When hot, fry the fillets for about 2 minutes on each side or until the skin is golden and the flesh has cooked all the way through. Add the capers, lemon juice and butter and heat through. Add the courgette flowers at the last minute so they are just wilted.

To serve, spoon some marmalade onto the centre of each plate and place a fish fillet on top. Pour the caper sauce over the fillet and arrange the courgette flowers around it.

FRIED SQUID RINGS WITH CAPERS AND POTATOES

Fusion chef Mónica Patiño astutely ups the squid ante here by fusing it with wine, punchy garlic, capers and chilli. The end result looks homely but conceals a sophisticated depth of flavours.

SERVES 6

- - - - - - - - -

750g (1lb 10oz) fresh squid rings

175g (6oz) plain flour

2 tbsp safflower oil

2 tbsp olive oil

5 garlic cloves, peeled and thinly sliced

350g (12oz) Cambray or small new potatoes, peeled, boiled and halved

6 *arbol* chillies, crushed

115g (4oz) small capers

300ml (10fl oz) white wine

700ml (1¼ pints) chicken stock

salt, pepper, chicken bouillon powder

juice of 2 lemons

1 tbsp chopped fresh parsley leaves

1 lemon, cut into 6 slices, to garnish

6 sprigs of fresh parsley, to garnish

6 *arbol* chillies, fried, to garnish

Lightly flour the squid rings and fry them briefly in hot safflower oil, then leave to drain in a colander.

Heat the olive oil in a large frying pan and fry the garlic until just golden. Add the potatoes, crushed chillies, capers and white wine and boil until the wine evaporates. Then pour in the chicken stock and bring back to the boil. Season with salt, pepper and chicken bouillon powder to taste.

Stir in the fried squid rings, lemon juice and parsley.

Serve in individual bowls, topped with a slice of lemon, a sprig of parsley and a fried *arbol* chilli.

ATÚN EN SALSA DE CHILE MORITA Y CAMARÓN

GRILLED TUNA IN PRAWN, PUMPKIN SEED AND *MORITA* CHILLI SAUCE

The *morita* chilli, despite its size, is a fiery one so you may want to reduce the quantity.

SERVES 6

1.25 kg (2lb 12oz) fresh tuna, cut into 6 fillets, about 200g (7oz) each

FOR THE MORITA CHILLI SAUCE

100g (3½oz) pumpkin seeds

55g (2oz) dried prawns

3 *morita* chillies

5 *hoja de aguacate* (Mexican or Haas avocado leaves*)

2 garlic cloves, peeled and crushed

3 tbsp olive oil

salt, to taste

* If unavailable, use 1 tsp of fennel seeds

In a frying pan, toast the pumpkin seeds, then add the prawns, *morita* chillies, *hoja de aguacate* and garlic. Add 600ml (1 pint) of water and cook for 5 minutes. Remove from the heat and pour into a food processor. Blend until smooth and strain.

Heat the oil in a frying pan and add the chilli sauce. Stir and heat through. Season with salt.

Grill the tuna fillets under a hot grill until cooked to your liking. Transfer to a serving plate and pour over the *morita* chilli sauce.

LINGUINI CON PULPO Y HONGOS SILVESTRES

LINGUINI WITH OCTOPUS, WILD MUSHROOMS AND SMOKED CHILLI

Pasta aficionados may be taken aback at the idea of reheating linguini, but the balance of flavours and textures is extraordinary – ever come across *mezcal* fighting for supremacy with chilli before? Just go with the flow!

SERVES 6

700g (1lb 9oz) linguini

1 onion, peeled

1 garlic clove, peeled and crushed

1 tsp dried *fines herbes*

2 tsp vegetable oil

salt, to taste

FOR THE SAUCE

100ml (3½fl oz) olive oil

800g (1lb 12oz) cooked octopus, chopped

100g (3½oz) wild mushrooms (*tecomate* or porcini), finely sliced

4 roasted *pasilla* chillies, deseeded and deveined

2 garlic cloves, peeled

150ml (5fl oz) white wine

50ml (2fl oz) *mezcal*

salt and freshly ground black pepper

Cook the linguini in plenty of boiling water with the onion, garlic, *fines herbes*, oil and a pinch of salt for about 10 minutes or until *al dente*. Drain, remove the onion and set aside.

While the pasta is cooking, make the sauce. Heat the olive oil in a frying pan, add the octopus and wild mushrooms and sauté until the mushrooms are tender.

In a blender or food processor, purée the chillies and garlic. Add to the octopus mixture in the frying pan.

Stir in the white wine and the *mezcal*, then add the linguini, toss well and heat through. Season with salt and pepper, then serve immediately.

CEVICHE MIXTO
MIXED SEAFOOD SALAD

**What better dish to share on a
hot day with a chilled Mexican beer
or two?**

SERVES 6

200g (7oz) cooked fresh crab meat or any very
    fresh fish

juice of 2 limes

1 bay leaf

salt and freshly ground black pepper

200g (7oz) fresh prawns, steamed for 5 minutes
    and shelled

200g (7oz) cooked octopus, chopped

1 plump tomato, diced

1 medium onion, peeled and finely chopped

½ avocado, peeled, stoned and finely chopped

small bunch of fresh coriander, finely chopped

chilli powder, to taste

1 lime, cut into 6 wedges, to garnish

taco chips (optional)

Put the crab meat in a non-metallic dish and
add the lime juice, bay leaf and salt and pepper.
Allow to marinate for 2–3 hours.

Mix the marinated crab, prawns, octopus,
tomato, onion and avocado together in a large
serving bowl. Stir in the coriander and the lime
juice marinade and season with salt, pepper
and chilli powder to taste. Decorate with the
lime wedges.

Serve slightly chilled with *taco* chips.

PEREJIL FRITO

FRIED PARSLEY WITH PRAWNS

The parsley in this starter contrasts splendidly with the juicy prawns, sharp lime and smoky flavour of the cream cheese dressing.

SERVES 4

2 large bunches fresh flat-leaf parsley

600ml (1 pint) vegetable oil

200g (7oz) bacon, diced

85g (3oz) cooked prawns

juice of 1 lime

salt, to taste

FOR THE CREAM CHEESE DRESSING

125g (4½oz) *chipotle* chilli salsa

350g (12oz) cream cheese

dash of soy sauce

dash of Worcestershire sauce

Rinse the parsley, remove the stems and pat dry. Fry in the hot oil over a high heat until golden. Remove from the oil, lay on paper towels to absorb the excess oil and set aside.

Fry the bacon in the same oil until just crisp. Remove from the pan and lay on paper towels to absorb the excess oil.

To make the cream cheese dressing, mix all the ingredients together.

To serve, arrange the parsley on a serving plate, top with the prawns and bacon, and drizzle with lime juice. Season with salt to taste and serve with the cream cheese dressing.

CARNE

MEAT

TACOS CON CHILORIO DE PATO

TACOS WITH SHREDDED DUCK AND ORANGE

This piquant recipe, from the food-rich region of Oaxaca, uses orange to allay the strong chilli and garlic flavours.

SERVES 6

50ml (2fl oz) vegetable oil

3 large onions, peeled and roughly chopped

3 garlic cloves, peeled and roughly chopped

150g (5½oz) *pasilla* chillies, roughly chopped

2 medium tomatoes, halved

1 tbsp Mexican orégano (or sage mixed with Italian oregano)

100ml (3½fl oz) white wine vinegar

300ml (10fl oz) fresh orange juice

salt and freshly ground black pepper

1 cooked duck, meat shredded

12 soft corn *tortillas*

2 large avocados, peeled, stoned and sliced, to garnish

In a frying pan, heat the oil, and sauté the onion, garlic and chillies until softened. Add the tomatoes and oregano and cook gently for about 15 minutes, stirring from time to time. Transfer to a food processor and blend to a purée.

Pour into a saucepan, stir in the vinegar and orange juice and warm over a low heat. Mix in the shredded duck meat, season with salt and pepper and simmer for about 10 minutes.

Heat the *tortillas* on a griddle or under the grill (they should stay soft, not crisp). Place a tablespoonful or two of the duck mixture along the centre of each, and fold in the sides to close. Serve garnished with avocado slices.

PECHUGA DE PATO CON TRES PURÉS
DUCK BREAST WITH THREE FRUIT PURÉES

Tender, slightly pink duck with flourishes of colourful purée, this is another work of art on a plate. Most of the elements can be prepared well in advance so it makes an excellent dinner party dish.

In a large bowl, mix the soy sauce, sesame oil, ginger, lemon and orange zests and salt to taste. Add the duck breasts, cover and marinate in the refrigerator for at least 2 hours.

For the orange zest confiture, pour 100ml (3½fl oz) of water into a saucepan and add the sugar. Bring to the boil and stir until the sugar is dissolved. Add the orange zest and simmer for 3–5 minutes. Strain and set aside.

Remove the duck breasts from the marinade, pat dry and fry in the oil in a hot frying pan until the skin is golden and the meat is cooked to taste – about 5 minutes on each side for pink, longer for more well done. Allow to sit for 5 minutes before serving.

Serve with smears of fruit purées, such as date, apple or tamarind on one side of the plate and arrange a duck breast on the opposite side. Add a spoonful of orange zest confiture, and garnish with a scattering of thyme leaves and a sprinkling of *fleur de sel*.

SERVES 4

200ml (7fl oz) soy sauce

4 tsp sesame oil

1 small piece fresh root ginger, peeled and finely chopped

zest of 1 lemon, roughly chopped

zest of 1 orange, roughly chopped

4 duck breasts, with skin on

salt, to taste

2 tbsp vegetable oil

fresh thyme leaves, to garnish

fleur de sel or coarse sea salt, to garnish

FOR THE ORANGE ZEST CONFITURE

100g (3½oz) caster sugar

zest of 1 orange, cut into fine strips

POC CHUC

GRILLED PORK IN ORANGE MARINADE

This divine Yucatecan classic is best served with hot corn *tortillas* and fiery *habanero* chillies. The sourness of the bitter orange works wonderfully with the pork, particularly when it is grilled over hot charcoal on a barbecue. Don't skip the side dishes, as they really complete the picture.

SERVES 6

900g (2lb) pork fillet

salt and freshly ground black pepper

1–2 garlic cloves, peeled and finely chopped

juice of 2 bitter oranges, such as Seville

2 bitter oranges, such as Seville, cut into
    quarters, to garnish

frijoles, to serve (see page 92)

FOR THE MARINATED RED ONION

400g (14oz) red onions

juice from 3 bitter oranges, such as Seville

bunch fresh coriander, chopped

salt, to taste

FOR THE CHILTOMATE (SALSA)

500g (1lb 2oz) tomatoes

1 small onion, peeled and finely chopped

small bunch of fresh coriander, finely chopped

salt, to taste

Season the pork fillet with salt and pepper and rub with the garlic. Cut into slices about 1cm (½in) thick. Arrange in a non-metallic dish and pour over the bitter orange juice. Cover and leave to stand for 1 hour.

To prepare the marinated onions, grill the whole onions on a hot griddle or under a hot grill, turning frequently until lightly browned all over. Leave to cool then peel and cut into 1cm (½in) pieces. Mix the onion with the bitter orange juice, coriander and salt, and set aside for about 1 hour.

To make the *chiltomate*, roast the tomatoes on a hot griddle or under the grill, turning frequently, then mash. Add the chopped onion, coriander and salt and set aside in the refrigerator.

Grill the pork fillets on a hot griddle, under a hot grill or over hot charcoal for about 4–5 minutes on each side or until just cooked.

Serve the fillets with the marinated red onion, *chiltomate* and *frijoles*. Garnish with orange wedges.

ASADO DE RES CON COSTRA

CRUSTED ROAST BEEF

Use top-quality organic beef for this, and serve it with an array of roasted vegetables to create a spectacular centrepiece for a dinner party. It is probably advisable to warn your guests that the crust harbours hidden heat from the chilli seeds.

SERVES 6

1.5kg (3lb 5oz) sirloin of beef

250ml (9fl oz) beef stock

FOR THE MARINADE

6 garlic cloves, peeled and crushed

1 small onion, peeled and finely chopped

1½ tbsp whole peppercorns

4 tbsp vegetable oil

2 tbsp white wine vinegar

5 tbsp chopped fresh oregano or
    rosemary (optional)

FOR THE CRUST

4 tbsp finely chopped fresh rosemary leaves

2 tbsp wheat germ

3 tbsp finely chopped roasted peanuts

1 tbsp chilli seeds

1 egg

salt and freshly ground black pepper

To prepare the marinade, pound the garlic, onion and peppercorns together in a mortar, then add the oil and vinegar. Blend well to form a paste, adding the herbs for greater depth of flavour.

Rub the marinade all over the beef and place it in a non-metallic dish. Cover with clingfilm and refrigerate overnight.

To make the crust, mix the rosemary, wheat germ, peanuts, chilli seeds and egg together in a bowl to form a stiff but malleable paste. Season with salt and pepper to taste.

Preheat the oven to 200°C/400°F/Gas 6.

Cover the beef with the crust mixture, pressing on firmly so that it stays in place. Put the beef on a rack in a shallow roasting tin and roast for 45 minutes for rare or longer if you prefer it more well done. Remove from the oven and leave to rest for about 8 minutes to let the meat relax and the juices flow.

Pour the stock into a saucepan and strain in the meat juices from the roasting tin. Bring to the boil over a high heat and reduce to thicken and form a gravy. Add a little salt if necessary. Pour over the slices of the beef and serve immediately.

VENADO AL ACHIOTE Y JUGO DE NARANJA CON ROMERO

VENISON IN *ACHIOTE*, ORANGE AND ROSEMARY SAUCE

Succulent and flavoursome venison, a typical pre-Hispanic meat, has made a big comeback among new-wave Mexican chefs as it is a lot less fatty than beef. Although deer are native to Mexico they are now protected, imported venison has to be used. Serve this with a pumpkin purée and fresh asparagus (when in season), or a simple green salad and potatoes.

SERVES 4

- - - - - - - - - -

100g (3½oz) *achiote* paste*

1 litre (1¾ pints) fresh orange juice

1 medium onion, peeled and sliced

1 garlic clove, peeled and crushed

1 sprig of fresh rosemary leaves, finely chopped

6 bay leaves

freshly ground black pepper

1 tsp sea salt

3 tbsp olive oil

1kg (2lb 4oz) loin of venison, in one piece

200g (7oz) butter

Preheat the oven to 230°C/450°F/Gas 8.

In a mixing bowl, whisk the *achiote* paste into the orange juice. Stir in the onion, garlic, rosemary, bay leaves, a twist of pepper and the salt.

In a large frying pan, heat the oil and sear the venison on all sides. Then transfer to a casserole and pour over the orange juice mixture. Bake for 10–15 minutes for rare, or 10–15 minutes longer if you prefer your meat well done. Remove the venison from the casserole and set aside.

Return the casserole to the oven, lower the heat to 180°C/350°F/Gas 4 and continue to cook the juices for another 30 minutes. Then strain the juice into a saucepan and boil over a medium heat until it is reduced by half. Adjust the seasoning if necessary and whisk in the butter.

Carve the venison into thin slices and quickly warm them up on a hot griddle or in a frying pan. Serve the meat bathed in the orange and rosemary sauce.

*If unavailable, mix ½ tsp cumin, 1 tsp paprika and 1 tsp oregano with 1 minced garlic clove and 1 tsp white wine vinegar and mix to form a paste.

PATO DORADITO CON SALSA DE MANGO
ROAST DUCK WITH MANGO SAUCE

Much of the success of this sweet-sour recipe depends on the mangoes. They should be very juicy and slightly soft but firm enough to retain their shape when cooked. The mango sauce can be prepared about 30 minutes before the ducks are ready. At the same time, steam some basmati rice as a simple complement to the complex flavours.

SERVES 4–6

2 × 2kg (4½lb) ducklings, roasted

FOR THE MANGO SAUCE

2 large green mangoes, about 700g
    (1lb 9oz)

2 tbsp brandy

3 tbsp caster sugar

1½ tsp finely chopped garlic

1 *arbol* chilli, finely chopped

1 tbsp finely chopped fresh root ginger

3 tbsp red wine vinegar

200ml (7fl oz) white wine

1 tbsp soy sauce

1 tbsp balsamic vinegar, or as needed

1 tbsp cornflour

coriander sprigs and fennel fronds, to garnish

Peel and cut the mangoes into bite-sized cubes, reserving their juice. Mix the juice with the brandy and marinate the mango in it for about 15 minutes.

Put two tablespoons of water in a large saucepan, add the sugar without stirring, then add the garlic, chilli and ginger.

Strain the mango, reserving the marinade, and add the fruit and red wine vinegar to the sugary water. Cover and warm over a low heat until the sugar dissolves. Do not stir.

Heat the white wine, add to the mango mixture and simmer to reduce the liquid by a third. The mango cubes should retain their shape. Add 250ml (8fl oz) of water and the soy sauce and, if necessary, adjust the sweet-sour flavour with the balsamic vinegar.

Mix the cornflour into the reserved mango marinade, pour into the mango mixture and stir around gently. Simmer until the liquid thickens slightly.

Carve the duckling, transfer to individual plates and pour some hot mango sauce over each portion. Garnish with coriander and fennel fronds.

CARNE APACHE
MICHOACÁN STEAK TARTARE

As one of Mexico's most rural states, Michoacán abounds with cowboys. They would love this dish as it is fresh, energizing and easy to prepare and to eat. Serve with toast or Mexican-style crackers, then hit the road.

SERVES 4

500g (1lb 2oz) good-quality organic lean minced beef

200ml (7fl oz) fresh lemon juice

150g (5¼oz) tomatoes, finely chopped

2 large onions, peeled and finely chopped

large bunch fresh coriander, finely chopped

55g (2oz) *serrano* chillies, deseeded, deveined and finely chopped

salt and freshly ground black pepper

1 ripe Hass avocado, peeled, stoned and sliced

Stir together the beef and the lemon juice in a non-metallic dish and leave to marinate for 15–20 minutes.

Stir in the tomatoes, onion, coriander and chillies. Season with salt and pepper.

Arrange on a plate and top with the avocado slices.

PATO EN SALSA DE CEREZA NEGRA

DUCK IN BLACK CHERRY SAUCE

This delicious recipe comes from Querétaro, a region where berries are abundant. Steamed in this way, the duck becomes ultra-tender. Serve it with wild rice and crunchy piles of finely sliced and sautéed leeks.

SERVES 4

1 duck, about 2 kg (4lb 4oz)

100ml (3½fl oz) vegetable oil

salt and freshly ground black pepper

2–3 tsp chopped fresh rosemary

100g (3½oz) carrots, peeled and cut into chunks

100g (3½oz) leeks, thickly sliced

100g (3½oz) celery, thickly sliced

2 medium onions, peeled and roughly chopped

FOR THE BLACK CHERRY SAUCE

500g (1lb 2oz) cranberry purée

2 tbsp brandy

250ml (9fl oz) red wine

100ml (3½fl oz) runny honey

300g (10½oz) pitted fresh black cherries

150ml (5fl oz) brown sauce

100g (3½oz) butter

Preheat oven to 200°C/400°F/Gas 6.

Wash the duck, pat dry with paper towels, then brush lightly with oil and sprinkle with salt, pepper and rosemary.

Arrange all the vegetables at the botton of a roasting tin and lay the duck on top. Pour 600ml (1 pint) of water into the roasting tin, cover with aluminum foil and place in the oven for about 3 hours.

Meanwhile, make the black cherry sauce. Heat the cranberry purée in a saucepan and flambé with the brandy. Add the wine, bring to the boil then stir in the honey and black cherries. Cook over a low heat for around 5 minutes until the cherries are hot and slightly softened. Stir in the brown sauce and butter and mix well.

To serve, carve the duck into four portions and serve on individual plates with the black cherry sauce poured on top.

PATO EN REDUCCIÓN DE CHALOTES, TOMILLO Y HONGOS SILVESTRES

DUCK WITH SHALLOTS, THYME AND WILD MUSHROOMS

Only the courageous would dare attempt this rather fiddly recipe, but the result is an exquisite *tour de force*. It needs to be prepared the day before.

SERVES 4-6

2 ducks, about 1.25 kg (2lb 1oz) each, cleaned

2 tbsp salt

10 sprigs of fresh thyme, leaves stripped off

4 tbsp olive oil

2 celery stalks, chopped

1 leek, chopped

500g (1lb 2oz) shallots, peeled and
   roughly chopped

500ml (18fl oz) chicken stock

12 small new potatoes, cut in half and parboiled
   for 10 minutes

225g (8oz) string beans, cut in half lengthways
   and parboiled for 3 minutes

12 wild mushrooms (*tecomate* or porcini)

salt and freshly ground black pepper

1 tbsp shredded *hoja santa*

Preheat the oven to 230°C/450°F/Gas 8. Rub the ducks with salt and a few thyme leaves. Roast for about 1 hour 50 minutes or until cooked through. Remove from the oven and leave to cool. Carefully pick the meat off the bones and refrigerate. Save the bones and wings.

In a large saucepan, heat 2 tablespoons of the oil and fry the duck bones and wings until they are golden, then add the celery, leek and shallots and fry for 10 minutes. Add 600ml (1 pint) of water, bring to the boil, and cook over medium heat until the liquid is reduced to a quarter of its original volume. Remove from the heat, strain, cool and refrigerate overnight.

Remove the grease that has risen to the top of the stock. Pour the stock into a saucepan and slowly bring to the boil. Add the remaining thyme and reduce the stock to a quarter of its original volume to create a rich sauce.

Preheat the oven to 200°C/400°F/Gas 6. Spread out the duck meat in a baking dish, and pour on the hot stock. Heat in the oven for 10 minutes.

Meanwhile, heat the remaining oil in a frying pan and fry the potatoes on their cut side until golden. Add the green beans and mushrooms and sauté until cooked. Season with salt and pepper to taste and sprinkle with *hoja santa*.

Serve the duck bathed in the sauce and accompanied by the potatoes, green beans and mushrooms.

POLLO ALCAPARRADO

CHICKEN WITH CAPERS

Native to the Yucatán, the *x'catik,* or *güero,* chilli pepper is long, lime green and very hot. If necessary, replace it with *habanero* but beware – either is pure fire! Otherwise, milder chillies will do. Here, the typically Yucatecan flavour of sour orange is countered by sweet raisins and sharp capers. It is quite delicious and an easy main course to serve for a dinner party.

SERVES 4

1 chicken, about 1kg (2lb 4oz)

55g (2oz) capers

juice of 5 peeled, bitter oranges such as Seville

2–3 garlic cloves, peeled and roasted

salt and freshly ground black pepper

1 tsp chicken boullion powder

2 tbsp vegetable oil

1 *x'catik (güero)* chilli, roasted

25g (1oz) pitted green olives

1 tbsp seedless raisins

200g (7oz) potatoes, peeled and quartered

1 onion, peeled, quartered and roasted

Joint the chicken into two breasts and two legs and place in a non-metallic dish.

Whiz half the capers and the orange juice in a blender or food processor. Add half the roasted garlic and season to taste with salt, pepper and boullion powder.

Pour over the chicken, cover and marinate in the refrigerator for at least 1 hour or up to 24 hours.

Heat the oil in a large saucepan. Remove the chicken pieces from the marinade, saving the liquid to use later. Pat the chicken dry with paper towels and fry until golden brown all over.

To the saucepan add 1 litre (1¾ pints) of water, the marinade and the roasted chilli, taking care not to break it open. Stir in the remaining capers, the olives and raisins and simmer, covered, for 10 minutes.

Add the potatoes, onion and the remaining garlic. Simmer, covered, for about 20 minutes or until the potatoes and chicken are cooked.

Divide the chicken pieces between four bowls and serve with the potatoes and a ladle or two of broth.

PAVO EN ESCABECHE ORIENTAL
MARINATED TURKEY IN SPICY ONION BROTH

You need to set aside an afternoon to prepare this, to allow for the marinating and the cooking time. It appears deceptively simple when cooked, however, and is usually served with white rice and *frijoles refritos*.

SERVES 6–8

1 turkey, about 4kg (9lb 3oz)

600ml (1 pint) fresh bitter orange juice, such as Seville

salt, to taste

2 tbsp olive oil

500g (1lb 2oz) onions, peeled and cut into strips

2–3 garlic cloves, peeled and crushed

5 *x'catik* (*güero*) chillies, roasted and chopped, or yellow cayenne pepper

FOR THE ESCABECHE (PICKLING SAUCE)

4 black peppercorns

5 cloves

1½ tsp freshly ground black pepper

½ tsp dried oregano

½ tsp cumin

5 garlic cloves, peeled

1½ tsp white wine vinegar or bitter orange juice

salt, to taste

Clean and season the turkey, joint into two breasts and two legs and place in a non-metallic dish.

To make the *escabeche*, grind all the ingredients together, except the salt and vinegar or orange juice, using a pestle and mortar and then sieve. Blend in the vinegar or orange juice to form a thick paste. Season with salt.

Stir 100g (3½oz) of the *escabeche* into the 600ml (1 pint) of bitter orange juice. Pour over the turkey joints and marinate for at least 2 hours.

Transfer the turkey and marinade to a large saucepan, pour in 1 litre (1¾ pints) of water and bring to the boil over a high heat. Reduce the heat to medium, cover with a lid and simmer for 2 hours.

Remove from the heat and leave to cool a little before lifting the turkey out of the saucepan. Cut or shred the turkey meat into small pieces. Strain the stock.

In a deep saucepan, heat the olive oil and sweat the onions and garlic over a low heat until softened. Add the chillies and turkey stock and bring to the boil. Stir in the shredded turkey, heat through and serve.

COCHINITA PIBIL
SLOW-BAKED PORK

Today's ovens cannot replicate the smoky, crisp finish of pork cooked in a *pib* – the stone-lined fire pit used by the Maya. But this is still a feast.

SERVES 8

1kg (2lb 4oz) boned shoulder or leg of pork, cut into bite-sized pieces

salt and freshly ground black pepper

2 garlic cloves, peeled and crushed

600ml (1 pint) fresh bitter orange juice

2 banana leaves or aluminum foil

2–3 tsp chopped fresh oregano

frijoles refritos, to serve (see page 92)

FOR THE ACHIOTE PASTE MARINADE

4 tbsp *achiote* seeds

1 tbsp chopped fresh oregano

1 tbsp cumin seeds

1½ tsp coarsely ground black pepper

12 peppercorns

10 garlic cloves, peeled

white wine vinegar or bitter orange juice

FOR THE MARINATED RED ONION

400g (14oz) red onions, peeled and chopped

juice of 3 peeled, bitter oranges such as Seville

salt, to taste

To make the *achiote* paste, put all the ingredients, except the vinegar or orange juice, in a food processor. Whiz to mix well, then, little by little, add just enough vinegar or orange juice to create a thick paste.

Season the pork with the salt and pepper and rub over the garlic.

Whisk the *achiote* paste into the orange juice and pour the mixture over the meat. Cover and leave to marinate in the refrigerator for at least 1 hour, or longer if possible (the longer, the better).

Preheat the oven to 200°C/400°C/Gas 6.

Place a banana leaf or a sheet of aluminum foil on the bottom of a baking dish, put the pork on top, sprinkle with oregano, then cover with the other banana leaf or another sheet of foil. Cover the dish tightly with a lid or with aluminum foil to prevent the steam from escaping and bake for at least 1 hour or until the pork is cooked through.

To prepare the marinated red onion, briefly blanch the onion in boiling water, then douse immediately in cold water and drain. Put in a non-metallic dish, pour over the orange juice, season with salt and set aside for about 1 hour.

Serve the pork with *frijoles refritos* (see page 92) and marinated red onion.

TZIC DE VENADO
SHREDDED VENISON

Deer used to be common in the Yucatán so venison crops up in many traditional recipes. This one is a light, chilled dish, ideal for lunch on a hot, sultry day. Serve on a wide platter with slices of avocado, tomato, lettuce and slivers of *habanero* chillies. *Frijoles* and warm *tortillas* are also classic accompaniments.

SERVES 4–6

1kg (2lb 4oz) venison , thickly sliced

salt and freshly ground black pepper

1 tsp dried oregano

banana leaves or aluminium foil

large bunch of radishes, finely sliced

large bunch of fresh coriander, finely chopped

1 small onion, peeled and finely chopped

juice of 4 bitter oranges (or juice of 2 oranges and 4 green limes)

1–2 bitter oranges, such as Seville, peeled and segmented, to garnish

Preheat the oven to 180°C/350°F/Gas 4. Season the venison with salt, pepper and oregano and lay on banana leaves or aluminium foil. Place in a roasting tin, cover with foil and bake for about 15 minutes until the meat has dried.

Remove from the oven, unwrap and shred finely.

In a large bowl, mix the shredded venison with the radishes, coriander and onion. Stir in the orange juice and season with salt. Refrigerate until cold.

Serve garnished with orange segments.

VERDURAS

VEGETABLES

TACOS DE QUELITES CON REQUESÓN
QUELITE AND RICOTTA *TACOS*

Quelites are wild greens and can be replaced with young spinach or watercress. The blue-corn tortilla adds a strong, rustic flavour. This recipe originated in Xochimilco, an area of waterways and floating gardens on the outskirts of Mexico City that is a relic of Aztec days.

Heat the oil in a heavy frying pan. Add the onion, garlic and chillies and fry gently until softened. Add the *quelites* and the ricotta and season with salt to taste. When the leaves have wilted, cover the frying pan with a lid and turn off the heat.

Mix all the ingredients for the *pico de gallo* together and set aside.

Just before serving the *tacos*, drain and discard the liquid that has been released from the *quelites*. Stir in the coriander and reheat gently.

Heat the *tortillas* quickly on both sides in a non-stick frying pan. Place about two tablespoons of filling in the centre of each and roll them up, leaving the ends open.

Serve immediately with the *pico de gallo* or a bowl of hot tomato sauce (see page 89).

SERVES 4–6

4 tbsp corn oil

1 medium onion, peeled and finely chopped

2 garlic cloves, peeled and finely chopped

2 green chillies, finely chopped

225g (8oz) *quelite* leaves, washed and dried

100g (3½oz) ricotta cheese

salt, to taste

4 tbsp finely chopped fresh coriander

12 blue-corn *tortillas*

FOR THE PICO DE GALLO (ORANGE AND TOMATO SALSA, LITERALLY 'ROOSTER'S BEAK')

2 oranges, peeled and segmented, pips removed

3 tbsp fresh lemon juice

½ onion, peeled and finely chopped

1 tomato, seeds removed and diced

3 *serrano* chillies, deseeded and deveined and finely diced

3 tbsp extra virgin olive oil

salt, to taste

BERENJENAS RELLENAS DE MANZANAS
BAKED AUBERGINES WITH APPLE STUFFING

Originally from Sinaloa, in northern Mexico, this makes a great vegetarian main course. It is extremely nutritious, substantial and full of flavour, especially with the hot tomato sauce.

SERVES 4

4 green apples, about 600g (1lb 5oz), peeled, cored and diced into 1cm (½in) cubes

2 tbsp fresh lemon juice

4 small aubergines, about 600g (1lb 5oz)

175ml (6fl oz) olive oil

1 small onion, peeled and finely chopped

2 garlic cloves, peeled and crushed

1 celery stalk, leaves removed, thinly sliced

4 tbsp wheat germ

24 fresh mint leaves, chopped

½ tsp cumin

½ tsp nutmeg

salt and freshly ground black pepper

4 tbsp butter

225g (8oz) Cheddar cheese, grated

FOR THE HOT TOMATO SAUCE

450g (1lb) plum tomatoes, roughly chopped

½ onion, peeled and finely chopped

5 *serrano* chillies, deseeded and deveined

salt, to taste

2 tbsp finely chopped fresh coriander

Preheat the oven to 200°C/400°F/Gas 6.

Toss the diced apple in the lemon juice. Cut the aubergines in half lengthways. Using a metal spoon, carefully scoop out all but 1cm (½in) of the pulp around the edge, taking care not to break the skin. Finely chop the pulp, mix with the apples and set aside.

In a large, heavy frying pan, heat the oil and gently fry the onion and garlic until softened, then add the celery, aubergine-apple mixture and wheat germ. Cook for 4 minutes, stirring all the time. Stir in the mint leaves, cumin and nutmeg, then season with salt and pepper to taste. Mix well and remove from the heat.

Grease a baking dish with butter. Arrange four aubergine shells in it. Divide the apple mixture between the four shells, then cover with the other aubergine halves. Bake for 15–20 minutes, until the aubergine is tender but firm.

To make the hot tomato sauce, put all the ingredients, except the coriander, in a pan with 2–3 tablespoons of water. Bring to a bubbling point, stirring frequently, and simmer for 10–12 minutes. Remove from the heat and allow to cool before blitzing in a blender or food processor. Strain and stir in the coriander.

Remove the aubergines from the oven, sprinkle the cheese over the top, and return to the oven for a few minutes until the cheese has melted. Reheat the tomato sauce, pour it into a serving dish and arrange the stuffed aubergines on top. Serve immediately.

QUESADILLAS ENTOMATADAS
TORTILLA ROLLS IN TOMATO

Excellent for lunch or as a starter, these *quesadillas* are one of Mexico's infinitely variable dishes. You can add cooked minced beef to make it a more substantial dish and some people like to pop it into a hot oven briefly to melt the cheese. What makes Flor's *quesadillas* extra special is the flavour of the fresh grilled tomatoes in the sauce.

SERVES 4

1kg (2lb 4oz) plum tomatoes

2–3 garlic cloves, peeled

1 medium onion, peeled and roughly chopped

12 corn *tortillas*

150ml (5fl oz) single cream

4–5 tbsp grated cheese, such as mature Cheddar

1 *jalapeño* chilli, to garnish

Grill the tomatoes, garlic and half of the chopped onion under a hot grill, turning frequently, for 15–20 minutes until the tomato skins are blackened. Peel away the charred areas then blitz the tomatoes, garlic and onion in a blender or food processor for a minute or so. Strain the resulting purée through a sieve.

On a hotplate or in a large frying pan, heat the *tortillas* in batches. A minute or so on each side is sufficient, as they must remain soft enough to roll. Alternatively, warm them up in a microwave for 1 minute.

Spoon some of the tomato sauce onto a plate, place a *tortilla* on top, cover it with more sauce, then roll up loosely. Repeat with two more *tortillas*. Drizzle with cream and sprinkle with the rest of the chopped onion and with the grated cheese. Top with a *jalapeño* chilli.

FRIJOLES

BLACK BEANS

Frijoles refritos **means 'refried beans';
in fact they are boiled, mashed, then
fried with chilli and onion. Like corn,
beans are one of Mexico's great
staples and passions. The red kidney
bean was their ancestor, cultivated
over 5000 years ago, but in Mayan
territory (also in the Caribbean) it is
the smaller black bean that wins over
hearts and palates. It is always cooked
with the herb** *epazote* **to reduce
flatulence, so beware. They can be
served unmashed, topped with
Parmesan and sour cream.**

SERVES 4

250g (9oz) black beans, rinsed, cleaned and
    soaked overnight or for 8 hours

1 handful of fresh *epazote*

1 small garlic clove, peeled and crushed

salt, to taste

1 tbsp vegetable oil

1 small onion, finely chopped

1 *x'catik* chilli

To make the *frijoles*, bring 1½litres (2¼ pints)
of water to the boil in a large saucepan. Drain
the soaking water from the beans and add
them to the saucepan of fresh water with the
epazote and garlic. Cover the saucepan with a lid
and simmer over a medium heat for 2½–3
hours or until the beans are tender. Add salt at
the end, when the beans begin to split open.
Drain and set aside.

Heat the oil in a frying pan then add the onion
and chilli and fry for 10–15 minutes. Add the
drained beans and cook for 5 minutes. Serve
hot, sprinkled with grated cheese.

CONVITES DULCES

SWEET TREATS

PIE CREMOSO DE LIMÓN VERDE, MERENGUE Y HELADO DE YOGURT

CREAMY LEMON MERINGUE PIE WITH YOGURT ICE CREAM

This wonderful dessert is an ironic take on the classic lemon meringue pie. All the ingredients are visible in an inside-out way, making it a perfect postmodern finale to dinner.

SERVES 4

3 egg whites

200g (7oz) caster sugar

175ml (6fl oz) sweet condensed milk

50ml (2fl oz) fresh lemon juice

200g (7oz) cream cheese

225g (8oz) María biscuits or any plain sweet biscuit, such as digestive or rich tea

250g (9oz) yogurt ice cream

finely grated zest of 1 lemon

Preheat the oven to 150°C/300°F/Gas 2.

Whisk the egg whites until stiff and forming peaks, then slowly add the sugar, whisking continuously. Line a baking tray with non-stick baking parchment and spread the meringue mixture thickly on top. Bake for 2 hours or until crisp. Turn off the oven and leave the meringue to cool in the oven until ready to use. Then break into bite-sized pieces.

In a bowl, beat the condensed milk and lemon juice until well blended and starting to thicken. Add the cream cheese and continue beating to form a smooth, thick cream. Refrigerate until well set.

Put the biscuits in a strong plastic bag and bash with a rolling pin, or blitz them in a food processor, until reduced to fine crumbs.

To serve, create a freestanding 'piece of pie' on each plate by arranging a triangular layer of biscuit crumbs as the base. Cover with the lemon cream crowned by pieces of meringue and a scoop of yogurt ice cream on the side. Finish with a sprinkling of lemon zest.

DULCE DE CAMOTE CON PIÑA
SWEET POTATO AND PINEAPPLE PURÉE

Typical of the cosmopolitan style in Veracruz, this sweet mash brings together sweet potato, originally from Africa, and pineapple, which the Spanish introduced from the Caribbean. It is delicious served with a dollop of crème fraîche.

SERVES 6

1kg (2lb 4oz) sweet potatoes, peeled, rinsed and roughly chopped

300g (10½oz) light soft brown sugar

4 thick slices of fresh pineapple, skin and core removed, roughly chopped (keeping some pieces back to garnish)

6 tbsp crème fraîche (optional)

In a large saucepan, cover the sweet potatoes with cold water and bring to the boil. When the water is bubbling, add the sugar and pineapple pieces and boil fast for 15–20 minutes, uncovered, or until the potatoes are soft and the liquid has partly reduced.

Strain and reserve the sweet cooking liquid. Give the pineapple and sweet potato a quick whiz in a blender or food processor, adding just enough of the cooking liquid to produce a smooth mash.

Serve warm or chilled in individual glasses, topped with a spoonful of crème fraîche and a few pineapple chunks.

FIG TARTS WITH PORT SAUCE

A sensational recipe, but complex to complete. If you can't find thyme ice cream, sprinkle chopped fresh thyme over vanilla ice cream instead.

To make the almond frangipani, beat the butter in a mixing bowl until smooth then whisk in the sugar and almonds. Continue to beat vigorously while gradually adding the egg and egg yolk, one at a time. Add the kirsch and almond extract and mix well.

Fold in the flour, then add the crème patissière and stir to blend well.

Place the pastry squares on a baking sheet and spread with a layer of frangipani. Arrange the fig halves on top and sprinkle with the vanilla sugar. Put in the freezer for 30 minutes to 1 hour, but no longer.

Preheat the oven to 200°C/400°F/Gas 6.

To prepare the port sauce, pour the port into a saucepan, add the sugar and boil until the mixture has reduced by at least a third.

Remove the tarts from the freezer and bake for 15 minutes. Remove from the oven and serve hot, topped with a scoop of thyme ice cream and a trickle of port sauce. If desired, decorate each plate with a swirl of vanilla custard, another of chocolate sauce and garnish with a sprig of thyme.

SERVES 6

450g (1lb) ready-rolled puff pastry, cut into 6 × 12cm (4½in) squares

1kg (2lb 4oz) fresh juicy figs, halved

175g (6oz) vanilla-flavoured sugar

350g (12oz) thyme ice cream

200ml (7oz) thin vanilla custard or best-quality ready-made custard

75ml (2½fl oz) chocolate sauce (optional)

thyme sprigs, to garnish

FOR THE ALMOND FRANGIPANI

3 tbsp butter, softened

3 tbsp caster sugar

3 tbsp ground almonds

1 large egg

1 egg yolk

1 tsp kirsch

⅛ tsp almond extract

1 tsp plain flour

40g (1½oz) crème patissière or best-quality ready-made custard

FOR THE PORT SAUCE

700ml (1¼ pints) port

500g (1lb 2oz) caster sugar

PAY MORELIANO

MORELIAN CHEESECAKE WITH GUAVA

María biscuits crop up quite often in Mexican recipes as they are the standard commercial brand. Use any plain sweet biscuit – rich tea or digestive – in their place. Guavas are popular in Michoacán and the subtly flavoured, jelly-like paste finds its way into numerous desserts.

Preheat the oven to 170°C/325°F/Gas 3.

To make the base, crush the biscuits to fine crumbs either in a food processor or by hand, in a plastic bag with a rolling pin. Mix in the butter and the egg. Press the mixture into the bottom of a buttered cake tin, 23cm (9in) in diameter.

Cover the crumb base with the pieces of guava paste.

Beat the remaining ingredients together until well blended. Pour over the biscuit and guava base. Bake for 25 minutes until lightly set.

Remove from oven and leave to cool before serving.

SERVES 8–10

FOR THE BASE

2 packets María biscuits, about 250g (9oz)

85g (3oz) butter, softened

1 large egg

FOR THE TOPPING

700g (1lb 9oz) roll of guava paste, chopped

200ml can condensed milk

100g (3½oz) cream cheese

4 large eggs

NATILLA CON VANILLA
VANILLA CREAM

During Easter week this dessert appears on every table in Mexico, but there's no reason not to make it throughout the year. Mexicans have a very sweet tooth, so you may want to reduce the sugar, but only use Muscovado, as it gives this dish a bittersweet kick.

SERVES 6–8

1 litre (1¾ pints) whole milk

1 vanilla pod, sliced lengthways with seeds left in

2 tbsp good-quality vanilla essence

200–250g (7–9oz) muscovado sugar

85g (3oz) cornflour mixed with 4 tbsp of cold water

55g (2oz) seedless raisins

In a saucepan, heat the milk, vanilla pod, vanilla essence and sugar very gently until just tepid.

Stir in the cornflour paste and keep stirring over a low heat as the mixture thickens until it comes to the boil.

Cool slightly before pouring into individual glass dishes. Chill in the refrigerator.

Scatter with some raisins before serving.

CHONGOS ZAMORANOS
MILK AND CINNAMON CREAM DESSERT

Ideally, *chongos* should be cooked in a *cazuela*, a traditional earthenware casserole that imparts a special flavour. This dessert is a much loved childhood pudding and exists in numerous canned versions, but this is the real thing.

SERVES 4–6

2 litres (3½ pints) whole milk

600g (1lb 5oz) caster sugar

6 drops of liquid rennet

100g (3½oz) cinnamon sticks, slivered

Pour the milk into a shallow, flameproof dish. Add the sugar and stir over a low heat until it has completely dissolved. Add the rennet, cover with a lid or some foil and set aside at room temperature for 2 hours until the mixture has set.

With a sharp knife, cut into 2.5–5cm (1–2in) squares in the dish and stick a sliver of cinnamon stick in each one.

Cook over a very low heat for 8 hours so that the milk caramelizes and turns golden. Cool before serving.

MOUSSE DE NARANJA Y MEZCAL
ORANGE MOUSSE WITH *MEZCAL*

Miguel Jiménez makes this divine mousse with mangoes only when they are in season as Mexican varieties are particularly sweet and juicy. Orange is a reliable substitute. You can use tequila instead of *mezcal*, though no self-respecting Oaxaqueño would do that. Miguel serves his mousse trickled with a reduction of red wine, simmered with sugar and a sprig of mint.

SERVES 4–6

7 large egg whites

400g (14oz) caster sugar

450ml (16fl oz) whipping cream

3 tbsp *mezcal* or tequila

600 ml (1 pint) fresh orange juice

25g (1oz) powdered gelatine

Whisk the egg whites until stiff, then gradually whisk in the sugar, one tablespoon at a time, to form a thick white meringue and set aside.

Whip the cream, slowly adding the *mezcal*, until it just holds soft peaks, then gently fold in the meringue.

Pour all but three tablespoons of the orange juice into a saucepan and heat until nearly boiling, then take off the heat. Soak the gelatine in the remaining orange juice then dissolve into the hot orange juice and leave to cool at room temperature.

Strain the orange jelly to remove any lumps and fold it gently into the whipped cream and meringue mixture. Pour into a glass dish and refrigerate for at least 4 hours or until set.

NICUATOLE
ZAPOTEC BLANCMANGE

Zapotec cook Abigail Mendoza's party dessert is made with flour from a very specific local corn. There is a touch of Italian *pannacotta* about its texture. The cochineal colouring she uses is the real thing, made from little beetles, the source of Europe's cardinal red dye in the 16th-century.

SERVES 6–8

700ml (1¼ pints) whole milk

200g (7oz) muscovado sugar

2 cinnamon sticks

200g (7oz) *masa harina* (Mexican corn flour)

cochineal or red colouring

In a large saucepan, mix 700ml (1¼ pints) of water with the milk, sugar and cinnamon. Slowly bring to the boil then add the *masa harina*, stirring continuously to blend thoroughly. Cook gently for about 1 hour over a low heat until thickened.

Pour two-thirds of the mixture into a deep, square serving dish. Mix a few drops of the colouring into the remaining mixture and pour on top. Cool and leave to set in the refrigerator, then cut into squares that will be part white, part pink. Serve in glass dishes.

ROLLO DE ATE Y QUESO
BAKED QUINCE AND CHEESE ROLLS

Morelia, where this recipe is from, is famous for its crystallized and preserved fruits found in incredible variety at the Mercado de Dulces (sweet market). Quince works perfectly with this recipe as its flavour marries so well with cheese.

SERVES 2–3

- 6 rectangular sheets of filo pastry roughly 16cm × 10cm (6¼in × 4in)
- 25g (1oz) butter, melted
- 150g (5½oz) quince paste
- 150g (5¼oz) fresh cheese such as feta, ricotta or soft goat's cheese
- 1 tbsp icing sugar

Preheat the oven to 200°C/400°F/Gas 6.

Brush the pastry sheets with half of the melted butter and spread a layer of quince paste over each, then cover with a layer of cheese. Roll up the pastry and place, seam-side down, on a baking sheet. Brush with the remaining melted butter and bake for 15–20 minutes.

To serve, make a few diagonal slashes in each roll and dust with a sifting of icing sugar.

BUÑUELOS CON MIEL DE PILONCILLO
DOUGHNUTS WITH BROWN SUGAR SYRUP

Piloncillo (unrefined sugar), sold in cones, is loved by Mexican cooks as it gives a natural sweetness that has far more flavour than refined white sugar. Muscovado sugar, with its high molasses content, comes very close.

SERVES 6

115g (4oz) plain flour

2 tsp caster sugar

1 tsp easy-blend dried yeast

pinch of salt

1 tbsp vegetable oil

2½ tbsp softened butter

250ml (9fl oz) vegetable oil

5 tbsp caster sugar

3 tbsp ground cinnamon

250g (9oz) fresh seasonal berries such as strawberries, raspberries or blueberries

FOR THE SUGAR LOAF SYRUP

125g (4½oz) sugar loaf or muscovado sugar

Pile up the flour on a large chopping board or clean work surface, or use a bowl if you prefer. Make a hollow in the middle and pour in the sugar, yeast, salt, oil and 50ml (2fl oz) of tepid water. Work the mixture with your hands, kneading well, until all the ingredients are thoroughly mixed and form a smooth ball of dough. Then work in the butter.

Divide the dough into 12 equal pieces. Roll each into a ball between your palms and flatten slightly into a round with a rolling pin. Line a baking tray with greaseproof paper and arrange the dough balls on top, leaving plenty of room between each one. Cover loosely with a sheet of oiled clingfilm and set aside in a warm place for 45–60 minutes until well-risen and almost doubled in size.

Meanwhile, make the syrup by dissolving the sugar in 250ml (9fl oz) of water over a low heat, simmering until the liquid thickens to a honey-like consistency.

Heat the oil in a large deep saucepan to a temperature of 160°C (325°F). Press your thumb into the centre of each dough ball to make a small indentation. Carefully fry a few dough balls at a time until golden. Lift out of the oil with a slotted spoon and lay on paper towels to absorb any excess oil.

Mix the sugar and cinnamon and toss the doughnuts in it until well coated.

Serve drizzled with syrup and scattered with fresh berries.

DULCE DE HIGOS VERDES
GREEN FIG DESSERT

As this Yucatecan dessert is extremely sweet, you may want to reduce the sugar slightly. You can also add curled strips of papaya to the figs. It is perfect after a light lunch, pre-siesta, with cicadas humming in the background.

SERVES 4–6

12 figs, firm inside but with soft skins

50ml (2fl oz) fresh lemon juice mixed with 50ml (2fl oz) water

375g (13oz) caster sugar

1 fig leaf

250ml (9fl oz) slightly sweetened whipped cream or crème fraiche

Boil the figs in water for 8 minutes. Drain and cool. Immerse in the lemon water and set aside.

Put the sugar and 350ml (12fl oz) of water in a large saucepan and heat, stirring continuously, until the sugar dissolves completely. Then boil, without stirring, for about 5 minutes to reach the light syrup stage.

Transfer the figs from the lemon water to the syrup and add the fig leaf. Simmer for 5 more minutes to thicken the syrup slightly.

Serve the figs in small dishes, doused in syrup and topped with a dollop of cream or crème fraîche.

TARTA DE LIMÓN CON NIEVE OAXAQUEÑA

LEMON TART WITH ROSE-PETAL ICE CREAM

Delicious and extremely pretty – this is a stylish end to any dinner party. Use any gently perfumed ice cream, maybe sprinkled with rose water and a few organic rose petals. With such crisp, paper-thin pastry, the emphasis is on the unctuous lemon filling.

SERVES 10

FOR THE PASTRY

250g (9oz) flour

25g (1oz) icing sugar

1 tsp salt

125g (4½oz) butter

1 egg yolk, beaten

FOR THE FILLING

10 eggs

400g (14oz) caster sugar

40g (1½oz) crème patissière or good-quality ready-made custard

200g (7fl oz) fresh lemon juice

300g (10½oz) butter, softened

rose-petal or other delicately scented ice cream

raspberry coulis

mint leaf, to garnish

wafer biscuit, to garnish

Preheat the oven to 200°C/400°F/Gas 6.

To make the pastry dough, mix the flour, sugar and salt together and form into a mound on a clean work surface or in a bowl, then make a well in the centre. Drop the butter into the hollow and rub into the dry ingredients with your fingertips to form fine, yellowish crumbs.

Form a well in the centre again and tip in the egg yolk and one tablespoon of cold water. Work the dry ingredients into the liquid, adding a little more water if required, to form a firm dough. Roll out the dough as thinly as possible.

Grease a large loose-bottomed flan tin and line it with the dough, covering the bottom and the sides. Prick the base with a fork, line with baking parchment and cover with baking beans. Bake for 15 minutes or until the pastry is lightly browned. Remove from the oven, allow to cool and refrigerate until ready to use.

To prepare the filling, beat the eggs, sugar, crème patissière and lemon juice until smooth and well blended. Pour into a non-stick saucepan and heat very gently, stirring continuously, to avoid scrambling the eggs. Then simmer and stir for 2 more minutes until thickened. Pour the mixture into a bowl and set aside to cool. When tepid, whisk in the butter. Pour into the pastry shell and refrigerate for at least 2 hours.

Serve with a scoop of rose-petal ice cream, or any other delicately scented ice cream, and a squiggle of raspberry coulis. Garnish with a mint leaf and wafer.

LAS BEBIDAS

DRINKS

AGUA DE JAMAICA CON CARICIA DE ROSAS

HIBISCUS FLOWER WATER WITH ROSE PETALS

Mexico's *aguas* (literally 'waters') are legion, found in every market and perfect for hot summer days. As the natural fruit juice is diluted with water and spiked with other flavours, it is extremely refreshing. Pure liquid poetry.

SERVES 4

250ml (9fl oz) hibiscus flower tea

175ml (6fl oz) natural syrup

5 tsp each cinnamon, clove and star aniseed herbal tea

700ml (1¼ pints) of mineral water

8 ice cubes, or to taste

edible rose petals, to garnish

zest of 1 lime, cut into matchsticks, to garnish (optional)

Mix all the ingredients in a glass pitcher and stir. Garnish with rose petals and lime matchsticks.

AGUA FRESCA DE LIMÓN CON HIERBABUENA

LEMON WATER WITH MINT

Nothing could be more refreshing than sharp lemon cut through with mint.

SERVES 4

24 large mint leaves

700ml (1¼ pints) mineral water, sparkling or still

125ml (4fl oz) lemon juice

125ml (4fl oz) natural syrup

8 ice cubes, or to taste

4 slices of lemon, to garnish

In a blender, whiz the mint leaves with 500ml (18fl oz) of the mineral water. Strain. Stir in the lemon juice, natural syrup and the rest of the water, then add the ice. Decorate each glass with a slice of lemon.

CAPPUCCINO DE FLOR DE CALABAZA
COURGETTE FLOWER CAPPUCCINO

This amusing variation on a well-known theme is an easy to prepare starter that slips down beautifully. Serve it in a glass coffee-cup or a simple glass bowl to show off the contents.

SERVES 4

1 tbsp olive oil

1 small onion, peeled and sliced

1 garlic clove, peeled and sliced

750g (1lb 10oz) courgette flowers or baby spinach leaves, rinsed

5 leaves fresh *epazote* or flat-leaf parsley

600ml (1 pint) milk

500ml (18fl oz) whipping cream

salt, to taste

freshly grated nutmeg

FOR THE COCONUT FOAM

250ml (9fl oz) coconut milk

Heat the olive oil in a saucepan and sauté the onion and garlic until softened. Tip in the courgette flowers or spinach and cook until wilted. Then add the *epazote*, milk and cream and simmer gently for 20 minutes. Salt to taste and blitz in a blender or food processor until smooth. Strain and set aside.

To prepare the coconut foam, heat the coconut milk in a saucepan until it begins to boil. Remove from the heat and beat vigorously with a hand-whisk until a foam forms, then allow to settle.

To serve, pour the hot 'cappuccino' into cups and spoon some coconut foam on top, using a slotted spoon. Sprinkle with a little grated nutmeg.

GLOSSARY

Achiote: annatto. Dark red seeds with woody flavour which produce scarlet colouring, popular in the Yucatán. A major part of *recado rojo*. Also comes as a paste.

Amaranto: amaranth. The seeds become a biscuit called *alegría* or are ground and added to corn flour and honey, or toasted and ground into gluten-free flour. High in protein, fibre and iron. Amaranth seeds should always be cooked because they block digestive uptake when raw.

Antojítos: 'little whims'. Mexican tapas or appetizers. A vast, ever-shifting category, they change name with regions and minor variations in form or filling. Basically a corn 'container' filled with delicious things, whether *taco*, *burrito*, *enchilada*, *chalupa*, *panucho*, *quesadilla* or *papdzul*.

Ceviche: marinated fish. Raw fish or shellfish marinated in lime juice with chilli, onion, garlic and coriander. Popular on the Pacific coast in Acapulco and the Gulf Coast in Veracruz and the Yucatán.

Chiles/Chillies: a digestive stimulant and an addiction, as they trigger endorphin 'highs'. Mexico grows around 150 types, from relatively mild *pasilla* and *ancho* to fiery *chipotle*, *cayenne* and *habanero*. Usually the larger ones are milder. Most of the heat is in the veins and seeds, which are unaffected by cooking or freezing. Buy plump, unwrinkled specimens. The usual way to cook chillies is to roast them over a flame until the skin is charred, then seal in a paper or plastic bag for 15 minutes or so to sweat. Hold under running cold water and flake off the burnt skin. Beware: your skin and eyes can burn from chilli juices so wash your hands after handling them. The best antidote is to soak your hands in milk or yogurt. The more capsaicin, the fierier the chilli. Capsaicin levels were first measured by Wilbur Lincoln Scoville (1865–1942), an American chemist who drew up a table of units. Below are the most commonly used Mexican chillies, though the world's hottest, *Naga Jolokia*, is Indian and shoots off the scale at over 1 million units.

bell pepper	0
anaheim	500 – 1,000
new mexico	500 – 1,000
ancho	1000 – 1500
mulato	1000 – 1500
pasilla	1000 – 1500
poblano	1000 – 1500
x'catic (güero)	2500 – 5000
guajillo	2500 – 5000
jalapeño	2500 – 5000
serrano	10,000 – 23,000
arbol	15,000 – 30,000
chipotle	15,000 – 30,000
morita	15,000 – 30,000
cayenne (tabasco)	30,000 – 50,000
piquin	50,000 – 100,000
habanero	100,000 – 350,000

Elote: cooked or canned sweetcorn, or barbecued corn-on-the-cob.

Epazote: wormseed. A strong aromatic wild herb often cooked with beans to reduce flatulence, also a remedy for intestinal disorders. Seeds and dried *epazote*, almost as good, are available by mail order. Mexicans swear by it.

Frijoles: beans. Mexico's 7000-year-old legume can be red kidney, pinto (speckled brown, the *refritos* classic), black (the Mayan favourite, cooked with *epazote*) or yellow.

Frijoles refritos: boiled beans mashed and fried with *piquin* chilli, a standard for *tortas* and *tacos* and with fried egg breakfasts. High in protein and carbohydrate and full of vitamins, minerals and fibre. Only add salt at the end of cooking or it takes twice as long for the beans to soften.

Hoja de aguacate: avocado leaf. Fresh or dried, they are used in soups, stews and with beans and can replace *hoja santa* in green *mole*.

Hoja santa/Hierba santa/Acuyo: a wonderful, anise-scented leaf often used for wrapping fish and *tamales* and in green *mole*. Grows in south-central Mexico. Big, about 20–25cm (8–10in), with a very special flavour.

Huitlacoche/Cuitlacoche: corn truffle. A fungus that grows naturally on ears of corn and has an earthy, smoky flavour. A great delicacy, often cooked with garlic and chilli for *tacos*, *tamales* and *quesadillas*. No one should be put off by the Nahuatl name, which means 'raven's excrement'. Outside Mexico, canned *huitlacoche* is available.

SUPPLIERS

Jícama: sometimes translated as yam bean or Mexican potato. This juicy tuber is similar to turnip and native to Mexico and California. The crisp, white flesh is eaten as a snack seasoned with chilli pepper, salt and lime juice.

Lima: Mexican lime (in Florida called key lime). Smaller, more fragrant and acidic, and thinner skinned than its Asian ancestor.

Masa harina: Mexican corn flour. The basis for *tortillas* and *tamales*. Aztecs, Zapotecs and Mayas all used the nixtamalization process, i.e. soaking and cooking dried corn kernels with lime or wood ash. This enhanced the nutritional value and also made it easier to grind.

Mole: Mexico's famously elaborate sauce, made to accompany turkey, chicken or pork, a moveable feast of ingredients (including dried fruit, nuts, spices, garlic, chillies, chocolate, shredded *tortilla*), cooked for several hours. Puebla and Oaxaca are the *mole* capitals, where there are countless variations.

Nopal: the leaf or paddle of the cactus that produces prickly pears. The spines are cut off and the leaf is sliced before being fried, grilled or roasted. It is very nutritious; high in calcium, fibre and vitamins A and C.

Orégano: Mexican oregano is used abundantly in the Yucatán. The subtle flavour resembles a mixture of sage and Italian oregano.

Recado: seasoning blends. The Yucatan's classic formula that comes in red (from the *achiote* seed), black (*chilmole*, from charred chillies) and green (from pumpkin seeds and oregano). *Recado para bistec* (for beef) contains black pepper, cinnamon and coriander seeds.

Tamales: the Nahuatl word *tamal* literally means 'wrapped', and that is what this ubiquitous *antojito* is, whether sweet or salty. Inside a dried corn husk or banana-leaf envelope is a soft corn dough filled with anything from turkey with *mole* to almonds and raisins – or even strawberries, allegedly another of Moctezuma's fancies. They are cooked by steaming and are a popular fiesta food with origins going back thousands of years.

Tomatillo: A small green fruit in a papery husk that has a tart edge, and is related to the Cape gooseberry. Canned and fresh *tomatillos* are available outside Mexico.

COOL CHILE CO
1 Enterprise Way
Triangle Business Centre
London NW10 6UG
Tel: 0870 902 1145 Fax: 0870 162 3923
Email: info@coolchile.co.uk
www.coolchile.co.uk
A pioneering company founded in 1993 with a great range. Also have a stall at Borough Market, south-east London.

EL AZTECA
164 Victoria Street
Victoria Village Shopping Centre
London SW1E 5LB (right in front of the station)
Tel: 020 7828 4937 / 07956 433029 / 07968 450568
www.elaztecafood.co.uk
Long-standing supplier catering to the Mexican expat community.

PEPPERS BY POST
Sea Spring Farm
West Bexington
Dorchester
Dorset DT2 9DD
Tel: 01308 897766 Fax: 01308 897735
Email: info@peppersbypost.biz
www.peppersbypost.biz
Mail-order freshly grown chillies and tomatillos.

MEX GROCER
Unit 17B Tollgate Farm
Tollgate Road
St. Albans AL4 0NY
Tel: 01727 569 010
www.mexgrocer.co.uk
Founded in 2006, with a large range of authentic Mexican ingredients and products.

CHEFS

Marcelino Avila, Celestún, Yucatan
It feels like the end of the line, a tiny,
ramshackle fishing village beside a
flamingo lagoon on the northwest corner
of the peninsula. But in among the
beach-restaurants is the eccentric
La Playita, where you can indulge in
Marcelino's divinely fresh seafood.
Or you could make his salad at home.
— *Mixed seafood salad* 58

Ruben and Adrian Cruz, Morelia
This father-and-son team run the
kitchens of La Azotea, a restaurant in
one of Morelia's top hotels, Los Juaninos.
Their creations combine culinary
experiments with tradition, but the
ingredients they use remain consistently
Mexican, if not always completely local
to Michoacán.
— *Baked quince & cheese rolls* 108
— *Doughnuts with brown sugar syrup* 109
— *Duck in black cherry sauce* 74
— *Mestizo soup* 41

Alicia Gironella de'Angeli, Mexico City
From her restaurant El Tajín in
bohemian-chic Coyoacán, Alicia Gironella
commands huge authority in the world of
Mexican food. Author of the Larousse of
Mexican cooking, she knows everything
about classic dishes, the most obscure
indigenous ingredients and works closely
with the Slow Food movement.
— *Crusted roast beef* 68
— *Quelite and ricotta tacos* 88
— *Sweet potato and chicken soup* 79

Martiniano ek Ayin, Mérida
In the early 1970s, Hacienda Teya, a
seventeenth-century landmark on the
historical and gastronomic map of the
Yucatán, became the first hacienda to
be converted into a hotel. The genial
Mayan chef, Martiniano ek Ayin, helped
to concoct its menu of exquisite
Yucatecan classics.
— *Chicken with capers* 79
— *Cream of coriander soup* 46
— *Grilled pork in orange marinade* 67
— *Lime and chicken broth* 42
— *Marinated turkey in spicy onion
  broth* 80
— *Slow-baked pork* 82

Alonso Hernández, Puebla
Hernández supervises the kitchens and
teaches cooking at Puebla's vividly pink
boutique hotel, Mesón de la Sacristía, the
perfect setting to promote authentic
Mexican cuisine. After studying chemical
engineering, Alonso decided to become
a chef, applying his love of alchemy to the
human palate.
— *Cream of bean soup* 36
— *Fried parsley with prawns* 60
— *Green pumpkin seed sauce* 27
— *Restorative chicken consommé* 44
— *Smoky Sacristia mole* 26
— *Tortilla and spicy beef snacks* 23
— *Traditional mole poblano* 24

Miguel Jiménez, Oaxaca
Together with executive chef, Juan
Pablo Luna, Miguel allows his culinary
imagination to run riot at Los Danzantes,
a convivial restaurant in central Oaxaca.
Local market produce and a Slow-Food
ethos fuse to create food fit for the gods.
— *Grilled tuna in prawn, pumpkin seed
  and morita chilli sauce* 56
— *Linguini with octopus, wild mushrooms
  and smoked chilli* 57
— *Orange mousse with mezcal* 104
— *Tacos with shredded duck and
  orange* 122

Victor Hugo Martínez, Morelia
While savouring his first chilli at the age of
four, Victor's taste buds and culinary
destiny were formed. One of ten children,
Victor Hugo learnt his craft helping his
mother, an education that he continued
by studying for a cookery diploma. His
passion for seafood and hot chilli shines
through in the recipes he has devised for
his restaurant, La Conspiración.
— *Marinated chilli prawns* 20
— *Michoacán steak tartare* 73
— *Tarascan chilli bean soup* 37

Abigail Mendoza, Oaxaca
Mendoza, an unforgettable, warm-
hearted Zapotec lady, lives in Teotitlán del
Valle, a famous weaving village of Oaxaca
Valley. Along with her sisters and nieces,
she runs an informal restaurant,
Tlamanalli, from inside her family's rug
workshop. The restaurant is famed for its
indigenous Oaxacan dishes.
— *Zapotec blancmange* 107

Enrique Olvera, Mexico City

Mexico's 'wunderkind', Enrique opened his first restaurant, Pujol in 2000 at the tender age of 24. Since then, his meteoric rise has secured its place on the list of the World's 50 Best restaurants. Trained at the Culinary Institute of New York, Olvera's approach is deconstructed and refined, yet also wholeheartedly Mexican.

— *Creamy lemon meringue pie with yogurt ice cream* 96
— *Duck breast with three fruit purées* 66
— *Prawn-filled avocado ravioli* 18

Martha Ortiz, Mexico City

With a character steeped in art, history and poetry, Martha Ortiz is Mexico's pasionaria of avant garde cuisine. Inspired by her artist-mother's cooking, her idiosyncratic dishes first appeared in 2002 at the much-applauded Aguila y Sol. She now sets a similarly imaginative tone at her restaurant, Dulce Patria.

— *Chilled cream of avocado soup* 32
— *'Nationalist' guacamole* 14

Mónica Patiño, Mexico City

Mexico City's serene superwoman, Mónica owns restaurants (including the celebrated Naos), hosts TV shows, writes cookery books, studies Buddhism, travels widely and has brought up four children. Long periods working in Asia and Europe have inspired her remarkable style of fusion cuisine.

— *Artichoke and clam soup* 34
— *Aubergine and goat's cheese mosaic* 28
— *Fig tarts with port sauce* 98
— *Fried squid rings with capers and potatoes* 55
— *Roast duck with mango sauce* 70

Flor Patricia Pérez, Veracruz

In Xico, a colourful town lost in the lush, coffee-growing hills of Veracruz, a modest little restaurant, La Fonda del Viejito, serves delectable local fare. This restaurant belongs to Flor Patricia, who learnt her skills in nearby Xalapa and is famed for her Veracruzan specials.

— *Seafood broth* 38
— *Spicy beans* 17
— *Sweet potato and pineapple purée* 97
— *Veracruz-style trout* 50

Alejandro Ruíz Olmedo, Oaxaca

Bubbling with enthusiasm and energy, Alejandro is immensely proud of his origins. He learnt to love food from his grandmother, in Oaxaca Valley and worked as a dishwasher and waiter before becoming a chef in Europe. He is widely admired for his creative, modern Mexican cuisine at Casa Oaxaca.

— *Broad bean soup* 45
— *Duck with shallots, thyme and wild mushrooms* 76
— *Fish fillet with lemon, capers and courgette flowers* 52
— *Tuna with soy sauce* 51
— *Venison in achiote, orange and rosemary sauce* 68

INDEX

ACKNOWLEDGEMENTS

Much of the impetus for this challenging project came from Manuel Díaz Cebrián, the dynamic head of the Mexican Tourist Office in London – to him a huge thank you, and also to Luis Rendón-Aguilar for his patience and logistical support, together with the Secretaria de Turismo in Mexico City.

Out there in that bewitching country of Mexico, my thanks go to all the chefs who collaborated so willingly, spared precious time and put up with our questions, cameras and appetites. How lucky I was to meet them and of course indulge in their divine dishes.

It was a pleasure to travel with my collaborators: Ana Sims, the recipe translator, who worked communication wonders, and Jean-Blaise Hall, the photographer, whose enthusiasm carried us through thick and thin. I shall always have fond memories too of the generous-spirited Mexicans encountered on the road, in kitchens and in markets.

Back in the UK, my thanks go to Alison Starling for initiating this edition of *¡Viva la Revolucion!* and to Jo Wilson for seeing the project through with such enthusiasm and thoughtfulness.

Deafening applause, too, for Juan Galindo, whom I consulted for his expertise on Mexican food, and for my old friend Jessica Johnson who introduced me to Mexico many aeons ago (in memory of VWs, pyramids, ant-bears and the like).

Finally, Richard: he knows how much I appreciate his constant support – but thank you.